About the Author

John Walker Pattison was born on Monday, 4th February 1957 to parents John and Ruby. He has lived most of his years in the wonderful seaside town of South Shields and enjoyed an uneventful, but happy childhood.

Today, Pattison enjoys being the practical joker, especially with his grandchildren. He openly admits to spending his school days clowning around and neglecting his intellectual chemistry, subsequently leaving school with a handful of worthless qualifications.

In 1973, he started work in a local shipyard until the spectre of cancer gripped his future in a deathly stranglehold. What happened next is his unique story, *Shadow of a Survivor*.

To the Oglala Lakota Sioux Nation, who unknowingly supported my psychological instability, providing untold inspiration during my most difficult times.

My wife June, not until fate brought us together did I discover who I truly was.

Donna Julie Pattison, your fight was my fight, and my success was your success. We overcame the odds together.

My family, and friends, both here and across the Atlantic Ocean, especially, James Glynn Poe — nothing is as important as family.

Space rock legends, Hawkwind – your music will always resonate in the canyons of my inner soul.

John Walker Pattison

SHADOW OF A SURVIVOR

Memoirs of a Cancer Survivor

AUSTIN MACAULEY PUBLISHERS

LONDON * CAMBRIDGE * NEW YORK * SHARJAH

A CIP catalogue record for this title is available from the British Library.

ISBN 9781037103032 (Paperback)
ISBN 9781037103049 (Hardback)
ISBN 9781037103056 (ePub e-book)

www.austinmacauley.com

First Published 2025
Austin Macauley Publishers Ltd®
1 Canada Square
Canary Wharf
London
E14 5AA

I would especially like to acknowledge all of the individuals whom I have had the honour and privilege of caring for during my career in Oncology and Haematology.

Chapter 1
The Irony of Reflection

The rain danced rhythmically against the windows, its soft cadence weaving seamlessly into the warm ambience of the lounge. I found myself lost in thought, reflecting on how life had changed in unimaginable ways. Next to me was June, my wife and partner of twenty-six years, whose smile and presence had been my constant source of comfort and joy.

The clink of glasses in the background seemed to punctuate my words. As the world outside pressed on with its endless demands, the chatter of other patrons faded into the background as my mind wandered back to a different time.

It was a typical February night, cold and dark, and the world was about to be thrust into turmoil as the Covid-19 pandemic loomed large. But that night, as I took a sip of my red wine, I felt contentment. For thirty-three years, I had dedicated my life to nursing in cancer services, a career filled with pride, challenges, and an overwhelming sense of purpose. I had spent decades caring for patients facing unimaginable hardships, yet despite the emotional toll, I cherished every moment. Furthermore, I thought of my grandchildren, the happiness of our marriage, and how life had been sweet, despite everything that had gone before.

It wasn't always like this. The boy I was in 1975 could never have imagined this life. Back then, sickness had overshadowed everything, every breath a struggle against the weight of an uncertain future. The hospital corridors, with their sterile walls and clinical smells, were my world.

Sitting there in the Cask Lounge, on that February night, I couldn't help but feel the strange twist of fate that had brought me full circle. This place had been witness to my evolution. Once it was a place I came to find solace, to escape the burden of my predicament. Now, it was a place of celebration, a symbol of how life had turned full circle. And here I was — no longer the sickly boy of 1975, fighting serious illness, but a man who had built a life filled with purpose, love, and a legacy I was proud of.

I raised my glass to take another sip, I smiled, realizing that life had its own way of surprising us. From the battle for my health to the beautiful life I had built, I had come far — further than I ever imagined possible.

How ironic, or was it just a strange twist of fate that multiple decades earlier, I stood right here, under very different circumstances, battling a crippling illness that threatened to rob me of any future.

In 1975, this was not a public house but part of the 'Town Hall Garage' selling a range of high-quality cars. At that time, I had a weekend ritual to follow. Each Saturday morning, irrespective of how I felt, I would take the bus ride to the garage to admire and covet the Datsun 280Z that had pride of place in the showroom. The black paintwork gleamed from every conceivable angle, yet at the same time, it reflected my forlorn image.

It was, of course, for sale, although the price tag meant nothing to me — I couldn't afford it, plain and simple. But it became my iconic motivation — that was, until other, more significant inspirations superseded it. I fantasized about owning that car every time I walked into that showroom, and those dreams were important.

I needed an incentive more than ever before, as I tried to come to terms with my illness. I desperately needed a focus that could guide me through the unforgiving ravages of chemotherapy treatment; something that could help me deal with the nightmare, although on many occasions I failed to deal with the uncompromising side effects of the brutal chemical prescription I was receiving.

Like anyone else, I could dream. But in all honesty, I needed to distance myself from the savage attack that threatened to usurp my physical and psychological well-being in unison. Each week, I would make the pilgrimage to the 'Town Hall Garage' just to admire this remarkable piece of machinery that realistically was way beyond my reach. It was quite simply escapism, a dream. But, importantly, at that time, it was an essential element of my coping mechanism.

My mind, still to this very day, will drift back to those dark times, subconsciously digging deep within my pockets to uncover repressed thoughts. So many difficult days when my mind would be clouded with fear and pessimism, days when my mortality was under threat by a denizen that came out of nowhere and over which, I had no control.

I can at least acknowledge now just how lucky, how fortunate I was to have survived what remains the most feared diagnosis known to society, a cancer diagnosis. Sadly, despite the advances made in treatments today, not everyone will be as fortunate as I have been.

As I lifted the red wine once more to my lips, and in the strangest twist of fate, my attention was quickly brought back to the present as the daily National Express London to South Shields bus cruised past. Ironically, only weeks before my ill-fated diagnosis, that very same daily express took me to London, and my very first adventure as an adolescent, a trip that would balance me onto the edge of danger.

My dreams, my aspirations, and my future would be turned upside down and inside out. The diagnosis I did not understand, the diagnosis that was divulged to my parents without my consent or knowledge — would shape my life in a way that I could never have imagined. My parents did all they could to shield me from the knowledge that the symptoms I experienced, and the investigations I had recently undergone, all came to the same conclusion, cancer.

They had decided that the best course of action was to keep that information from me. How they planned to do so when I was facing not months but years of chemotherapy and radiotherapy will forever remain a mystery. Whilst I cannot condone their attempted secrecy, I fully understand their desire to protect their only son, as there is no worse feeling in the world than being told that your child has cancer.

I was about to embark on a journey of unrivalled proportions, a pathway that was beyond my comprehension and understanding and more importantly, was beyond my control. Yet, strangely, it would be the journey that shaped me into the person I am today. Perhaps even a better person than I might have become, had cancer not shattered my life and influenced the tapestry of my life.

This journey would take me to the very edge of existence. On more than one occasion, I would stare the grim reaper in the face, be delivered to death's door, only to find that there was no one at home to take me in. Chemical messengers would attack my body from every conceivable angle in an attempt to rid my body of its unwanted assailant. A poison that knew no compassion.

Chemotherapy would snatch my innocence, and my naivety, leaving me weak, vulnerable and, on more than one occasion, ready to submit. Perhaps the pivotal moment that was instrumental in changing the direction of my life took place within the confines of a busy cancer ward at Newcastle General Hospital in 1976.

My cancer diagnosis had been established twelve months earlier, and the effects of cycle after cycle of chemotherapy that had been pumped into my accommodating veins rendered me completely demoralized by the onslaught of the barbaric medicine. As I saw it, the savagery of chemotherapy and its unrelenting side effects had led to a daily psychological battle that I seemed to be losing.

I had been receiving treatment for more than a year. Despite my physical and psychological struggle to accept the diagnosis and tolerate the chemotherapy, it had all been in vain as it proved, not for the first time, to be unsuccessful. I am informed that the cancer was progressing. I was emotionally unstable, and I felt defeated, completely fatigued, tearful and ready to capitulate. I could take no more…

There was only so much one person could take. Like an immature teenager, I felt I had reached my limit; quite simply, I could take no more of this unbiased attack that was beginning to destroy my mind and was eroding my sanity.

I made my decision. I would accept no more of the barbarous treatment, and just allow fate to take its course, whatever the consequence of this action may be.

Deep down, I knew what this decision meant, as tears rolled down my cheeks and, being at perhaps the lowest point since diagnosis, I momentarily contemplated suicide. But then, in a rational moment, I thought of the consequences that would have on my parents.

A hidden veil of unanswered questions pestered my subconscious mind every hour of every day. Self-posed questions of mortality and survival raised emotions so diverse and unknown to my immature mind, and caused such fear that my tentative optimism was indiscriminately cast aside and replaced by indecision and doubt.

Where was my support, who, if anyone, could help when I was dying of cancer? I awoke each morning and went to bed every night with these thoughts, created by an unwanted accomplice. I was fearful of the permanent psychological damage the disease was causing. The mental distress aside, chemotherapy had already inflicted pain and indiscriminate harm physically, and my fragile body of less than seven stone was struggling to recover.

Having already endured many months of the unforgiving brutality of chemotherapy and, now, I am told that my cancer has not been halted despite all of that ferocious treatment that I had accepted for almost a year. During chemotherapy, I had struggled mentally and physically to deal with the persistent barrage of side effects, and my inability to accept the uncertainty that went hand in hand with this cruel diagnosis.

Following my first relapse, I knew my life was balanced on a knife-edge; the persistent temptation of suicide was never far away, luring me towards its irreversible embrace.

The conflict that many cancer patients harbour in the remote depths of their minds, the time we all fear had arrived. I was ready to accept the consequences of ending my treatment.

It was a fact that my body was gripped by cancer, and which was unwilling to release its deathly stranglehold. I was aware of what the outcome of my action would be, yet paradoxically I was relieved that from somewhere, and I have no idea where, I summoned the courage to make that choice — no more chemotherapy. I felt broken, weak and subverted by illness, defeated by my diagnosis, unable to take another step forward on the uneven road of the cancer journey.

In reality, it wasn't just the physical destruction caused by a malignant disease that I objected to. It was also the fact that it was eating into my very soul, sowing seeds of doubt within my mind and interfering with every element of my existence. Slowly but surely, it was leaving a permanent, and an unseen reminder, a deep, hidden scar, and a legacy, which, if I were fortunate enough to survive, would last forever.

So, a confrontation between me, an immature and terrified teenager and a young Nurse called Syd would be a moment of pivotal change, and a defining instance in my young life. A moment that was destined to occur, and I believe a consequence of fate. I was young, defiant, confused, and angry and once I set my mind to do something, it would be a brave nurse who would attempt to intervene, and change that decision, regardless of how well-intentioned their actions were.

However, with true compassion, empathy, and a dogged determination not to stand back and watch me throw my life away, Syd did exactly that, intervened. He told me what I already knew, that without the treatment I would die. My tearful counterargument didn't deter him and, eventually, his support, persuasion, and understanding led me to reverse my decision not to have more treatment.

His fervent optimism was admirable, and yet he did not glory in his success. Had we not had that conversation, the story would have ended here. Instead, it was the beginning of a lifelong cancer journey that would take me through many new and unknown dimensions in my life, a pathway of self-discovery, and learning.

As a consequence, my association with cancer would be a unique, and unparalleled journey that was destined to influence so many dimensions of not just my life but others along the way. Today, fifty years later, it continues to be a significant component in my life; without the cancer experience, I would not be the person I am today; a better person, a philosophical soul, determined to contribute to the ongoing needs of all those affected by the most feared diagnosis known to society, cancer.

My story is intended to be an insight into my challenges, my anxieties, and one of the greatest confrontations known to society, the fight against cancer.

However, my story is different to many others because it didn't just continue to be my fight. Documenting my experience has been cathartic, and I sincerely hope reading this account will help others who have been touched in some way, shape, or form by the condition to which medical science still has little or no answer.

We all respond in different ways to the pressure and emotions, the fears and the stigma that this disease can elicit and no textbook or professional can tell you what the correct response is. Statistically, there is a one in two chance of being given a cancer diagnosis at some point during a lifetime. Cancer probably affects everyone in society to some extent as we all know someone, friend or loved one who has been diagnosed with this feared illness.

This survivorship chronicle is my personal story, my journal of events and coping strategies. The highs, and the many lows of my cancer journey and undoubtedly, it will be very different to every other individual who has been touched by cancer. There are no correct or incorrect responses to the brutality that is brought about by a cancer diagnosis. It is very much an individual response and undoubtedly, it will initiate a whole myriad of different and instinctive responses in each person that it impacts.

Emotions do not follow a pre-arranged script when attacked by the turmoil of malignant disease. The confusion inflicted on the mind, and the desire to rid the body of this unwanted accomplice, is one of the hardest issues to deal with. The feelings of helplessness and despair are at times almost constant companions, yet at other times the pleasure and sanctity of life give you an unexpected determination to battle on.

The fear and emotional retribution cancer brought gave me an appreciation of life that would otherwise have been missing, although it took me some time to realize how sweet and important life truly was and remains. At this early point, it would be wrong not to pay tribute and acknowledge the love that I received from my family, my parents and, of course, my dearest sister, Allyson, but also an extended family of aunts and uncles.

In many respects, my diagnosis allowed me to discover myself and appreciate the wonders of life. But there were times when my anger at the diagnosis meant that I would resent life itself and question, more than once, my very own existence. On more than just an isolated occasion, I would ask myself whether this fight to survive was worth it.

The darkness that lurked in the canyons of my mind, always attempting to befriend me, caused a pathological resentment that was stronger on some days than others. Darkness that offered its cruel hand and, yet thankfully, I did not have the courage or the heart to step forward and grip that handshake, a handshake that would have terminated my life.

The trauma of fighting tooth, and nail to beat the demon that is cancer has been instrumental in making me who I am today. I make no apology for repeating this. But there have been many other experiences that have helped me to discover who I am, and who John Walker Pattison is and has become.

My life to date has, at times, been difficult, but it has also been one of pleasing discovery and I would not, in hindsight, change any of it. Perhaps other than the heartache of a failed marriage and the unnecessary retributions it brought. I certainly feel fortunate for the way my life was mapped out by fate, and my experiences to date have allowed me to appreciate all that is good and worthwhile in life itself.

Malignant disease has played a significant part in my life and has presented many difficult, and life-changing challenges, but, hard as it is to understand, many positives came from that. It caused me to reflect on what is, and what is not, relevant in my life. This enabled me to recognize the difficulty other individuals face and find the strength, like so many others, to overcome adversity and to look forward to tomorrow.

My story deals with the effects of not only the disease and its treatments, but also its long-term effects and how I cope with the permanent legacy of cancer survivorship. It is also about the harrowing dilemma I faced as the father of a daughter given the diagnosis of terminal leukaemia. Strangely, I firmly believe that cancer has given me a virtue that would have been absent had the disease not touched my very existence and threatened it more than once.

Life is a privilege for all of us. You cannot put a price on life and health; they are invaluable and precious and deserve to be respected. Sadly, for many people, it is often the onset of an illness, or the death of a loved one, which brings that into focus. A cancer diagnosis certainly influences your approach to life, your philosophical beliefs and all that you represent and believe. In that respect, I am no doubt, like all other cancer patients, reflective, philosophical, grateful and respectful of a condition that society fears more than any other.

However, not everyone affected by cancer will come up with the same answers. All of us, whether a patient, a parent, a partner or significant other, will have a different perspective on the many perplexing challenges that life puts in front of us. The huge challenges that cancer throws at us, the numerous dilemmas we face, and that are instigated by such a terrible disease, undoubtedly, in my opinion, influence our philosophy, and beliefs.

It would seem appropriate, therefore, to describe a few of my early encounters. Delivering an insight into my character, and how it was before the spectre of cancer consumed my adolescence, and then moulded my personality into what it is today.

The challenges of a cancer diagnosis, both physical and psychological, remain the same today as they did at the time of my diagnosis. But cancer is so much more than a psychological and physical challenge, it is also a challenge financially, but importantly, it affects the remainder of your life. For those fortunate enough to survive, then that legacy is ever-present and is now, at last, recognized by the health care establishment as such.

Today, five decades on, I can reflect on my diagnosis, my survival and how I stared death squarely in the face. I can see the difficult pathway of life that I had to navigate multiple decades earlier. The melancholy I now feel, yet also the strange sense of catharsis and most importantly, ironically, gratitude at how life has treated me.

Reflecting on the real possibility of an early death at such a young age makes it easier to accept chronic ill health today, ill health that is a consequence of the salubrious chemotherapy and radiotherapy delivered fifty years ago.

Unexpectedly surviving when the medical staff told my parents, I would not. Overcoming all the odds, I am now humbled to be one of the longest-living cancer survivors in the UK today and so, this is my story...

Chapter 2
It's Only Rock and Roll

My story began when Ruby and John announced the arrival of their first child, John Walker Pattison on Monday, 4 February 1957. I was born in South Shields, a small seaside town nestling on the North East coast of England. My father was a plumber working along the banks of the River Tyne, and my mother managed the household as was the tradition at that time — in later years, she would work several part-time jobs.

I would be joined four years later by a sister, Allyson Mary. My childhood was uneventful, and happy. As a youngster, I enjoyed all that life had to offer, football, fishing and finding trouble, the latter being the easiest to achieve, and something I excelled at.

As an independent twelve-year-old, I attended my first football match in September 1969 to watch Newcastle United. Despite the team losing 1-0 to Derby County, my passion for football was ignited. I still remember handing over my silver coin and pushing through the clackerty-clack of the iron turnstiles.

Climbing the concrete stairs, I was greeted by the lush green turf and the roar of forty thousand Geordies awaiting their heroes — a moment that stays with you forever. My spine tingled as the teams marched onto the field and the game got underway. Today, as a season ticket holder, my commitment to the black-and-white army remains unwavering, bringing both immense joy and endless frustration over the years.

Like most schoolboys, I once dreamed of playing for the Magpies. Realistically, though, many of my classmates were far more skilled. I played a few games for the school team, and whenever I did, my father was my biggest supporter — though more often than not, I found myself shivering on the touchline as a substitute.

Football may have been my first love, but music soon became my greatest inspiration. Not just any music, but the kind that resonated deep within me, shaping my life and fuelling my adolescent years — an adolescence marked by both physical trauma and emotional pain greater than any work of fiction.

I would describe myself as an animated extrovert, easy-going, and opinionated yet open-minded. Philosophical at times, I respect the views of others even when I disagree — and if I do, I'll tell you. But I never hold grudges; life is too short for that. I take great pride in my family and my hometown of South Shields.

During my early years, music became an obsession, consuming my attention and pushing aside nearly everything else, including my education. At fifteen, I discovered a band called Hawkwind — still in the early stages of their journey — and from that moment, my world would never be the same.

The band was formed in the late sixties by a former street busker, and they played what was described as '*space rock*,' which I immediately identified with. A raw mixture of electronics, guitars and a hypnotic beat of percussion; all blended into the musical equation, of an inventive light show with saxophone and an exotic dancer!

It was a Neanderthal approach to music that influenced the way so many other bands deliver their music, and it continues to do so even today. The band played many venues the length, and breadth of the country, and many of these gigs were free shows, often supporting worthy charitable causes. Sadly for me, however, a young fifteen-year-old, I had to be content with their records, and the regular news articles in the national music journals.

I did not, at that particular juncture in time, realize just how influential and motivational Hawkwind would become as my health deteriorated, and how they would unknowingly support me through a psychological battle unlike any other. I would go on to need other motivational influences at different times in my life, some as dependable as Hawkwind and some, far more so.

My connection to the band was far more than a fleeting adolescent obsession — it was a lifeline. Through the darkest depths of depression, the relentless side effects of aggressive chemotherapy, and the mind-numbing struggle to cope with the reality of facing an early death, I found solace in the music of Hawkwind. Their sound became my escape, carrying me beyond my pain and fear, if only for a little while.

In my formative years, I would be the first to admit that my school years were wasted. I did not study as I should have, and I treated my education as a trivial escapade. Life is there to be enjoyed, and I felt education was getting in the way of my enjoyment of life. My best friend at the time, Alan Robertson, known as Robbo, was just as crazy as I was.

If we weren't at one another's house watching such comedy greats as Spike Milligan or Monty Python's Flying Circus; then we'd be preparing to play some outlandish practical joke on friends, much to their disgust, and often anger. Classmates would avoid us when we were seen together, knowing that we aimed to create pranks that gave us so much satisfaction.

Robbo and I both enjoyed our music, and like so many, it was always our intention to become rock stars. True to this lifestyle, I had been letting my hair grow for some time, this would be my statement, my identity, my freedom; in part, my rebellion.

In 1972, a year when The New Seekers, and Donny Osmond would both top the charts, life was all about music for me, but not pop music, space rock was my chosen genre. At night, five or six of us would meet after school and quite innocently walk the streets listening to our music on a cassette player. It was harmless entertainment, and it kept us out of trouble.

Thursday and Friday nights were youth club nights. At St Hilda's, most Friday nights, there would be a disco and occasionally a live band. The youth club was an excellent place to network. But the good thing about these discos was that around 9 p.m. the DJ would play a rock slot with around half a dozen well-established rock tracks, such as Deep Purple, Black Sabbath and Led Zeppelin.

Occasionally, I would convince the disc jockey to play a Hawkwind track, when they did, it would almost always be '**Silver Machine**' as this had been a huge chart success for the band, peaking at number three in 1972. Once I heard the tell-tale sound of its introduction, I would bounce onto the dance floor.

Most often, there would only be a couple of us who would venture onto the dance floor during the rock session; although occasionally, a couple of the girls might also join in, their motivation was one of pure ridicule. But, nothing would have stopped me from dancing once Hawkwind was playing, as I saw my attempts at creative dance as a tribute to the band I now revered.

During that time, I met Dave, a dedicated Status Quo fan, and he also felt that when his band played, he should be there on the dance floor. Subsequently, each Friday, once the rock session was underway, we would seek each other out as if we had a secret mission to accomplish, dancing. Dave became a lifelong dependable friend, and I was honoured to be his best man, not once but twice.

There were many anecdotal stories about those early days and the mischief I regularly found, most often, of course, I didn't have to look far for it, trouble seemed as though it could find me easily. Having previously admitted to wasting my school years, I subsequently left school with a handful of worthless qualifications.

In later years, I would make up for this lack of educational ambition, after having learned some valuable lessons about life. It had always been my ambition to follow my father into plumbing, but due to my poor exam achievements, I was unlikely to be offered an apprenticeship in that trade.

As a young man, I admit to being rather immature, and I think this was almost certainly a legacy of my wasted schooling, although I would also make up for this later on in life. I do believe that fate governs our lives. When we are born, we are dealt a hand of cards, and we have no option other than to play that hand of cards in the game known as life.

That's putting things simply; of course, I do not believe that you can change your fate, call it destiny if you like. However, you can tempt fate by your actions. I firmly believe that life is mapped out for us all. And I believe my fate was mapped out, and being a scholar in those early days was not part of it.

Sometime towards the end of August 1973, my father and I headed across to the North-side of the River Tyne, where interviews were being held for apprenticeships in a number of the local shipyards. Shipbuilding and coal mining had been the mainstay of employment in the area for many decades.

The River Tyne has always been recognized as the world capital of Shipbuilding, having produced quality and famous ships for centuries, including the first of the supertankers, naval vessels by the score, including HMS Ark Royal and HMS Illustrious. In fact, I had a secret hankering to join the Royal Navy at some point.

Sadly, today, that industry in the North East has almost all but disappeared.

During my interview, I sat nervously, fidgeting from side to side. The interviewer sat quietly, checking out the meagre qualifications that I had proudly presented to him, before offering me an apprenticeship as a Welder. I was quite naive but also bewildered as to why I could not be a plumber, but realizing that I had to map out a career of some description and secure a financial future for myself, I accepted the apprenticeship.

It was better than nothing and the pay wasn't too bad, which was an important issue. Dad had explained the necessity of taking up such a post and I respected his view; therefore, in a few moments, the indentures were signed. I was on the first rung of the employment ladder, but what an ascent that would turn out to be.

And so it was that I had secured my first position of employment and the prospect of life as a Welder. The first twelve-month were spent in a training school starting only a few weeks later. My first pay packet of £9.97 filled me with excitement, as I now could realize one of my very first dreams, to see Hawkwind live.

Late in 1973, Sound's music paper advertised what for me would be an exceptional event, the next Hawkwind tour, just what I had desperately been waiting for. To my great disappointment, I found, on closer scrutiny of their tour dates, that there was no Newcastle gig, even though they were playing just about every other corner of the country.

I was determined not to miss an opportunity to see them, so there was only one thing for it, if they were not to visit the North East, then I would have to travel elsewhere to see them. Subsequently, I decided to see them at the now legendary Edmonton Sundown in London early in the New Year of 74.

On my return from work that night I sent off my postal order and a stamped addressed envelope for the most important ticket of my life; the life that would take so many twists and turns, deliver so much heartache and yet provide untold experiences, both good and bad.

My ticket duly arrived, and I recall with crystal clarity, just gazing at the maroon coloured ticket before leaving for work on that November morning. I could hardly believe that on 26 January 1974, I would, at last, get to see Hawkwind live and my first encounter with the big city.

At the same time, the experience of working life in the training school revealed many new dimensions of social activity.

A number of the other apprentices had girlfriends and amazed me with some of their tales and escapades. It proved to demonstrate my innocence and naivety, and that I had lots to learn, not only about girls but also about life in general. However, girls were never high on my agenda, like most young lads I'd had some girlfriends, but only one proved serious for me, and that was Lauren, the Mayor's daughter.

I fell in love with her the first time I set eyes upon her. I summoned the courage to ask her out, though not personally, as that was too embarrassing. Instead, one of the guys asked her on my behalf, and I was amazed when she said yes. Sadly, after a brief courtship, she ended the relationship, which broke my heart into a thousand pieces.

My youthful looks often proved a hindrance. Rarely, if ever, could I walk into a bar and get served without being questioned about my age and whether I was even allowed to be there. It was, of course, embarrassing. To avoid the scrutiny, I would slip into a quiet corner, out of sight of the landlord, and pass my cash to someone else to buy my drinks.

The very first time I recall doing this, was in the Albemarle in 1973, a popular bar in South Shields town centre. I crept into the corner of the room and handed over my fifty pence to Alan, enough for four pints of Newcastle Exhibition beer. I felt like a man, and also one of the crowd, but at the end of the night, I was so drunk that I could barely walk, and found myself staggering to and fro as if marching across the deck of a ship in a gale-force wind.

'Get the fool into a taxi,' was the call from one of the lads. Once home, despite my drunken stupor, I recall stumbling across the doorway, only to be faced with the mammoth task of ascending the stairs. I was up three steps and back down two, until eventually, I collapsed on top of my bed; the horrendous experience of the room spinning before I dropped off to sleep, and waking the next morning with the hangover from hell.

My first thought was, never again, something most of us have said before, not until the next time that is. Though they never said anything, I'm sure my parents knew that I was drunk. Parents just know these things, don't they?

Life in a shipyard brought many more friends, and many more adventures. I was a typical teenager, dabbling in all that teenagers do, which included my first experience of cannabis and acid (LSD). After all, it was the acid-drenched seventies. I was never into the drug scene heavily, but in an honest account of the influential changes I have experienced, I admit it did play a small part, and I do not intend to hide or falsify any aspect of what is written here.

The time had come to make my long-awaited trip to London, and the following week I made the eight-hour journey to London by National Express Coach. Foolishly, I had not been as sensible as to arrange accommodation for my visit to the capital; I thought that I would surely be able to arrange something when I got there?

Eventually, I arrived in the Capital, and as I had not been to London previously, I had little idea as to which direction to head in my attempt to find the arena.

A few hours later, after much searching and inquiring, I found myself outside the venue. I had time to spare and got myself something to eat before making my way into the auditorium, just as the support band was coming on stage, Global Village Trucking Company, if I recall correctly. This was just incredible, what an atmosphere, was I about to see Hawkwind after waiting so long?

The air was filled with the sweet smell of cannabis, but my adrenaline was flowing, and I was on an artificial high of natural endorphins and euphoria. Eventually, Hawkwind took to the stage and the crowd erupted, the hairs on the back of my neck stood to attention, as the band welcomed everyone to the Sundown. Hawkwind then exploded into their first number, '**Brainbox Pollution**.'

I was mesmerized; they continued their set and played without a pause between songs. Behind the band, there was a giant screen onto, which animated images were projected representing each of the songs being delivered to the admiring audience. As they played, an astonishing light show lit up the whole front of the stage, making the performance even more dramatic.

What an experience, what a show, the gig was spectacular, much more than even I had expected, and in honesty, there aren't enough adjectives in my vocabulary to explain the brilliance of the show. I was speechless, and impressed as never before. At the end of the performance, the crowd exploded with appreciation as the band left the stage, only to return minutes later to deliver an explosive encore, their final number being '**Silver Machine**.'

That night was something else, something I cannot explain, something that will live with me for the rest of my life, something only a Hawkwind fan can appreciate. All too soon, the show was over and reluctant to leave, I resentfully made my way out of the arena and through the streets of Brixton still buzzing with excitement and delirium. I felt like I was floating through deep space, and without the need for an artificial substance.

My desire to see more of the band was, simply, insatiable. As I walked through the streets of London, the people passing by probably thought I was crazy, smiling to myself one moment, then remembering the song list, and singing away to myself the next. Who needed drugs when such a rush could be gained in this way?

Unknowingly, I was about to fall to earth with a heavy bump. I was about to encounter a problem later that cold January night. During that fantastic Hawkwind concert, I had had the good fortune to meet countless like-minded people, several Scottish guys who, like me, had travelled down to the concert by coach, a journey they had made previously.

They were extremely friendly, and had told me that as their coach, like mine, wasn't due to leave until the next morning — they had planned to allow themselves to be locked into Euston Station so that they could sleep there. This idea didn't fill me with much inspiration, although I was tempted, and in hindsight, I should have allowed my temptation to rule; instead, I decided to make my way back to Victoria Coach Station.

I had been told that, provided you had a valid ticket of travel, you could sleep on one of the overnight-parked buses. It was now well after midnight, and a handful of coaches were parked indiscriminately in the now desolate station. I found the coach that a few others had already boarded, and I climbed aboard, and secured one of the many empty seats.

Seated for around thirty minutes, there were probably only half a dozen other people on the bus with the same intent as I or so I thought. I felt fairly comfortable with my legs tucked up covered with my Afghan coat, that was until two adults, and a young girl got onto the coach. I assumed that all three were together, but unfortunately, I could not have been more wrong.

The lady and her daughter sat two rows behind me, and the man sat next to me despite, all the other empty seats. I thought it odd but, in my naivety, I didn't question this, thinking that all three were together. When only a few moments passed, his hand brushed against my knee. In my continued naivety, I thought that this was an accident, and I pushed away his arm.

Sadly, I was very wrong, and immediately his hand took a firm grip on my left leg. Realizing with alarm what was happening, I immediately jumped to my feet, and forced my way past this pervert, and headed off the bus. The man remained firmly implanted in his seat, as I took one final backwards glance.

Now shaking, and frightened, I walked briskly out of Victoria Coach Station and wondered what to do on this extremely bitter January night, a hard frost now covering the ground. Dressed only in jeans, a t-shirt, and an Afghan coat, my hands felt numb from the brisk cold winter wind. Thankfully, I discovered the Salvation Army soup kitchen, and made the best of what had been a disturbing event.

Fortunately, the incident did not detract from my enjoyment of finally seeing Hawkwind live, and early the following day, I jumped on the bus to head back to South Shields. Now, eager to tell my friends of the brilliant performance I had at last witnessed. But, having now experienced Hawkwind live, this was never going to be enough of this visually stunning and amazing psychedelic band.

Hawkwind offered something no other band could deliver; the unique blend of space rock, a spectacular light show and even an exotic dancer, the fantasy of many a young man. For me, travelling around the country to see Hawkwind would almost become a full-time career; in fact, I always had aspirations of joining the band as one of the road crew — would that be part of my fate?

Sadly, that was never to be. Perhaps if illness had not intervened then that dream might have come to fruition, who knows? Instead, I had to make do with seeing the band play at many venues around this great country of ours. It also allowed me to make friends with other like-minded individuals.

Back at home and acknowledging that the current Hawkwind tour was in full swing, I browsed the tour itinerary posted on my bedroom wall and I noticed they were to play Leeds University in mid-February. There was no reason why I couldn't make the relatively short trip to Leeds to see that performance too. Life was good; life could not get any better, but it could certainly get worse!

Returning from Leeds, I was feeling exhausted. I was now enjoying life more than ever and felt this fatigue was due to my travels. It was a Friday, downstairs in the Ship and Royal was not only the place where the local rockers met, but it was also the venue where various drugs were exchanged for cash.

Equally, I will not try to justify, or argue the case for drug-taking but, for me and the circle of friends I associated with, Cannabis was smoked on a regular occurrence. I only took LSD on a handful of occasions, probably only because of the as yet unknown intervention of illness. As a believer in fate, I would argue that things happen for a reason and, therefore, had it not been for the intervention of cancer, then illegal drugs may well have destroyed my life at a relatively young age.

Friends at work had similar tastes in rock music and subsequently invited me to join them at their local pub. Evenings at the Marsden Inn would become an important social event on most nights of the week; I now had a group of friends with whom I could readily identify. They enjoyed my kind of music, and we would take in regular live bands at various venues around the region.

Saturday night was a rock disco at the Commando in South Shields, an upstairs room in a dishevelled pub, threadbare carpets covered the floor and the sweet smell of hashish filled the air. Many rockers who attended the Commando were indeed into stronger drugs, such as Cocaine and even heroin.

Significantly, however, despite being an impressionable and immature teenager, I was consciously aware these were not for me, and I can honestly say that I was never tempted to try these harder, potentially addictive substances. Despite being embraced into their fold for almost a year, I would, unfortunately, lose contact with my newfound fraternity, but not by choice.

I had other friends, of course, but they had different priorities than I did and most importantly, they did not share my passion for rock music. Some of the guys I knew had some musical talent, significantly more than I did. They had decided to form a band, and had invited me to be the roadie and arrange the sound system and, quite naturally, I jumped at the chance, recognizing this could be my first opportunity to begin a life of rock and roll.

They had named themselves 'Shelter' and after some months of impromptu rehearsals an agent arranged their first gig at a local workingman's club. This could be the first tentative step to rock stardom, and I was part of it. Life was moving in a direction that gave me great pleasure; sadly, however, something was lurking just around the corner, which would soon put a stop to my current enjoyment and which would take my life in a different and unexpected direction.

The band felt as prepared as they could be, and so we hastily crammed the musical equipment into the back of a beat-up Transit van, which had definitely seen better days, and headed down the A19. Having no vehicle of our own, we managed to persuade its owner to transport us to this most important event, hopefully, the first of many gigs to come.

The show was at Shiney Row Club, and on the night, everyone was on a high as we set up the stage, ready to be on stage at 8.00 p.m. Naturally, being their debut, the lads were nervous and consumed a few beers. Before we knew it, the master of ceremonies came on stage, stood to attention behind his microphone, and said, 'Please give a massive welcome for Shelter.'

Rapturous applause came from the unsuspecting audience, who sat back in eager anticipation. The agent who had booked the gig had informed the band that this was a 'rock night,' which, as it turned out, could not have been further from the truth. The lads marched onto the stage like proud gladiators being welcomed into the Roman Coliseum; they quickly armed themselves with the appropriate musical instruments and then blasted out the guitar riff introduction to '**Johnny 'B' Goode.**'

The lead singer jumped around the stage like a contorted epileptic, writhing and twisting before the first words came from his youthful throat. At the end of this number, the singer was puffing and panting, and I was doubtful whether he had the stamina for the rest of the show. The audience were not impressed, and it was clear from their muffled grunts and groans that they weren't expecting a 'rock night!' but something more like 'Darby and Joan.'

Still, in true show business fashion, the lads were determined to carry on their distinguished performance. Unfortunately, their second song — an Allman Brothers Band number — proved just as unpopular as the first. Without hesitation, the compère rushed onto the stage, swiftly bringing an end to both the boys' performance and the noise they had so proudly delivered.

I can't remember his exact words, but the message was crystal clear. '*Get off*!'

Needless to say, the boy's embarrassment was sky-high, and they refused to go back on stage to clear away the equipment; instead, that was left to me and the other roadie. It was an unnerving experience, clearing the stage to the ogling eyes of two hundred beer-swilling pensioners.

One of the lads, Ralph, was so embarrassed that instead of leaving the building, by the way we had entered, and he decided to climb from the dressing room window and into the awaiting transit van. Meeting with Ralph some thirty years later, he would profess to still be mentally scarred from that experience.

On the way home we had a good laugh about the entire experience and looked forward to the next gig, although at that time I was unaware that that would be my first and last gig with the boys, but not by choice.

There were many escapades in the shipyards too, and it was remarkable that ships got built. One chap called Plank; I'll let you decide why this was his name, let's just say, he was not the brightest bulb in the box. He would often fall asleep during an afternoon break and, on one occasion, we welded the steel caps of his boots to the deck of the ship, and left him to awaken in surprise. Another character was Irish; he was an apprentice burner, and was supposed to be burning something off the inside of the ship's shell.

Unfortunately, he burned through the wrong area of the shell, causing water to seep into where he was working. He was not popular when the foreman discovered his mistake, and that's putting it mildly. I was seventeen and enjoying life fully. If this was what life was all about, having fun and following Hawkwind from tour to tour, then life was sweet.

My goal at that moment was to get backstage, and meet the band during their next tour. That was going to be a difficult feat, and it was, but for a reason, I did not expect. The band had recently released their new album 'Hall of the

Mountain Grill' and one particular track was exceptional, packed with emotion, and incorporating haunting keyboards.

It immediately became a favourite of mine; in fact, it remains a favourite to this day. It was called '**Wind of Change**' and paradoxically, that's precisely what I was about to experience.

Hawkwind had already completed a successful tour of America earlier in the year, and now they were on the road again in the United Kingdom. They were scheduled to perform in the North East on the 12 December, and this time, I would get to see them at Newcastle City Hall, as I would in the following years.

Sure enough, 12 December would be a fantastic gig, if anything; they were much improved from earlier in the year. Two days later, I travelled to Manchester to witness the band at the Palace, and at that moment, life could not have been any better. Yes, life was cool, what more could a young man want from his existence?

Had I not needed the commitment of work to finance my following of Hawkwind, then I would have simply made sure that I attended each show in each city of each tour. In April of the following year, I decided to make the journey down to Dunstable, London to see Hawkwind before they started to tour America later that same year. On the 13 April 1975, in complete innocence of what lay ahead, I travelled to Dunstable and the Queensway Hall.

Sadly, after a long and exhausting journey, I felt the performance on this occasion was not the power-packed space rock that I was becoming accustomed to, it seemed a somewhat indifferent performance, but perhaps it was me. During the show, I was unable to maintain a steady degree of concentration and my enthusiasm was waning, not for the band, far from it, it was more my physical well-being as my vigour seemed to be draining from my body.

I had no idea what was causing my fatigue, other than perhaps the long and tiring journey to Dunstable. Despite my weariness, I felt that my long trek south had not been in vain, I still had aspirations to join the band in some shape or form and understood that not every performance would be great, although the onset of my extreme tiredness still puzzled me; my exhaustion was overpowering, and I was subdued by its superior force.

When I returned to work, I was still exuberant from the gig. I was slowly but surely beginning to realize that this fatigue had been consuming me physically for many weeks. I had been feeling decidedly weak, even during my trip to

Dunstable, I hadn't felt well and in hindsight, it was the euphoria of the gig and seeing Hawkwind live that had masked the overwhelming malaise.

I recalled that only weeks before my trip, I had been struggling to motivate myself to go out after work, and on most nights, I'd go straight home, eat with the family, and then fall asleep in front of the fire. However, such was my enthusiasm to share my experiences of the concert that I did return to work following the Dunstable gig. Unknown to me, that would be my last day at work for some time.

It was becoming increasingly difficult to motivate myself. At times, I was struggling to breathe, and it seemed that all I ever did was sleep. In addition, I had lost a significant amount of weight, but out of nothing besides ignorance, I had no concern about this, even though at that time I weighed just a little over seven stones.

Other symptoms included drenching night sweats that were so profuse that the entire bedding had to be changed. I had developed an intractable cough, which would eventually; once I was admitted to the hospital, require Methadone to settle it.

In addition, I had also developed breasts, medically known as gynaecomastia, admittedly only small ones but again, out of naivety, I thought nothing of it. Furthermore, slowly but surely, my skin was taking on a yellow tinge called jaundice.

By this time, I had already made several visits to my family doctor, but he was about as much use as a chocolate fireguard, insisting that I was depressed, and prescribed anti-depressants, Valium to be exact. I did not think I was depressed, quite the opposite in fact, but if the doctor said that's what it was, who was I to argue?

Each meal became a battle, the inevitable sickness following with relentless force. Nausea was my constant companion, a dull ache in the pit of my stomach that never truly faded. Every step I took felt heavier than the last, weighed down by an exhaustion so deep it seeped into my bones. My legs, though capable, betrayed me with weakness and a strange tingling, as if warning me of something I could not yet name.

The fatigue was more than tiredness — it was suffocating, an invisible force pressing down on me, draining me even in moments of stillness. No amount of rest brought relief. My body was failing me, and I didn't know why. Sick days piled up, yet I forced myself to work. The Shipyards were unforgiving, and some managers ruled as if their authority was life itself. But no one, not even they, could understand the war I was fighting within myself.

They looked down on everyone with pure contempt, as if authority gave them the right to bully, belittle, and humiliate. Because of them, most managers carried a bad reputation — some unfairly, others deservedly so. For those who thrived on power, the position was a perfect excuse to intimidate and degrade.

But not all of them. Some played fair. As long as you did your work, they left you alone.

For me, though, none of it mattered. I was eighteen, reckless, and saw life as one big joke. Rules, authority, expectations — I laughed them off. And because of that, I clashed with managers constantly, always finding myself in the middle of some argument or another.

Chapter 3
Collusion is a Dirty Word

May 1975 was the month Led Zeppelin returned to England to play five sold-out shows at Earls Court in London. West Ham United won the FA Cup, beating Fulham two goals to nil, and Vauxhall launched the Chevette, a small hatchback car. Only two months earlier, the Netherlands had won the Eurovision Song Contest with '**Ding a Dong**,' while the ageless, Shadows were admirable runners-up.

It was also the time when my life would change forever, marking the beginning of an experience that would not only manipulate my philosophy but develop my inner strength. It would also make me realize something I'd never been aware of before; that my own mental and physical weaknesses were vulnerable. What I was about to experience would change my approach to every day for the remainder of my life.

This was my fate. The experience was to make such radical alterations to my mindset that, although I didn't know it at that time, I would eventually become eternally grateful. I was about to embark upon a positively reflective journey. I was about to step onto a treacherous pathway of unknown proportions, and a perilous journey of self-discovery.

There were periods of hope and optimism but, at the same time, there were moments when I experienced the darkest of nightmares unrivalled by any work of fiction. I was unaware that this forthcoming pathway would take me to the very edge of sanity, and threaten my existence.

Generally, I was happy, despite the unexplainable lethargy that dominated my every breath. The situation had now been going on for some weeks and the family doctor appeared to be none the wiser as to the origins of my current symptoms and was unconcerned. If he was not concerned, then surely I should not be either, and I thought it would correct itself soon.

Yet despite that exhaustion, I managed to function — only a few weeks earlier I had dragged myself to the last game of the football season to see Newcastle United deliver a lack-lustre performance, and to be beaten by Birmingham City, finishing a disappointing fifteenth in Division one.

Despite my ongoing optimism of recovery from this inexplicable exhaustion, on an occasional night, I would be taunted by the thought that I would live with this unwanted fatigue forever. Despite my exhaustion, I still retained my interest in Hawkwind, and they had yet another new album out called 'Warrior on the Edge of Time,' which proved a real masterpiece. How ironic that very soon I would feel as if I were the one on the edge of time, perilously balanced between life and death.

With an effort that was becoming increasingly difficult to muster, I was dragging myself out of bed each morning to try to persuade myself into work. One particular day, I was allocated a job in the cofferdams. These are the structures within the bowels of the ship, similar to the honeycomb structure of a beehive. The job would entail me physically dragging the welding cable down through the seemingly hundreds of manholes and into the double bottoms.

Naturally, there was no lighting down there, and it was my responsibility to take a lamp with me so that the specific area could be illuminated. Trust me when I say, these cofferdams were well named; they were frightening places, black and deadly silent.

After dragging the cable down to the bowels of the ship, I was overcome with exhaustion and felt I couldn't breathe. I, therefore, decided to sit and have a short rest before starting the welding job expected of me. It was now around eleven in the morning and not surprisingly, as you might expect, such was my fatigue that I fell sound asleep, well, it couldn't harm to have a short nap, could it?

Some three hours later and I was awoken by one hell of a bang, my Manager had found me asleep. The siren had signalled lunch and everyone had gone for their break and then duly returned to work. Everyone, except for me, and of course, this had not gone unnoticed. Jimmy was my manager, and he had come looking to see what kind of progress had been made with the job, although as far as he was concerned I had gone absent without leave.

Imagine his anger when he made the difficult journey into the cofferdams and found me sleeping like a newborn baby. Luckily for me, Jimmy wasn't a bad Manager, there were many much worse. What followed was a fierce verbal rebuke, and yet I knew I'd got off lightly; many other managers would have sacked me there and then.

The following day to my verbal rollicking, I simply could not get out of bed as my weakness was getting steadily worse following another drenching night of sweats. No sooner did I stand up, the little energy I did have seemed to evaporate within seconds.

It made no sense, and I was not strong enough to fight it, so I simply lay back down on the wet bedding. The night sweats were a specific symptom and caused such a degree of soaking that the bed looked as if someone had thrown a bucket of water over it.

Mum was working at the Scarlet Coat, a local and well-respected restaurant, and knew I was too unwell to go to work, and instead of hauling my weak frame down to the doctors in person, she insisted on a home visit. I agreed with her and later that morning the doctor arrived and immediately decided to have me admitted to the local hospital.

He suggested that my problem was not depression after all, but probably appendicitis, which would require an operation. This was quite a change from his original diagnosis and yet, he was still way off target with this new diagnosis. He then insisted on calling an ambulance and a blue light flashed me past the almost stationary traffic towards the Ingham Infirmary.

The first investigation was a simple blood test, although this would be the first of many. Several hours later a blood transfusion was arranged for me as it had been discovered that I was anaemic, a typical presentation of many cancers, although that word was not mentioned yet. Eventually, the doctor came along and placed a needle into the back of my hand without any explanation of the intended intervention, nor did he ask for my consent.

Soon afterward, the nurse arrived at my bedside holding the bag of red fluid. That same night, some friends came in to visit me and attempted to make fun of the situation, but such was my weakness that I could not get motivated by their attempts at joviality and found little fun in their antics, no matter how well-intentioned. Still, it was nice that they had made the effort to come and see me. Well, for now anyway!

Blood test followed blood test, followed by an x-ray, then the poking and prodding under my arms, squeezing my neck, then a hand on my stomach and a stethoscope on my chest and then on my back. Physical examination became a daily routine for several doctors and, of course, more blood tests. Despite the almost constant investigations in those early days, I recall that they were long, lonely, and painful days.

On occasions, I thought that my body was no longer mine; such was the intensity of the constant intervention, the prodding and poking and the ongoing barrage of the same questions made me feel as if they were designed to catch me out. Did they not believe what I had already told them? I vividly remember lying in a side room in the Ingham Infirmary with my radio playing and of course, regardless of which station I chose, there would be no Hawkwind.

Instead, I had to make do with commercial radio playing pop music; however, it served to break the monotony of those long, tiresome days in what for me felt like solitary confinement. As if it were yesterday, I vividly recall the record, '**Loving You**' by Minnie Rippiton being aired. That song seemed to be on every station at ten-minute intervals, and it drove me to despair.

Even today, if I hear it, there is a negative association with those dark and dismal days. What others might consider being a triviality, in that situation, feeling so desperately low, I felt that the disc jockey on whatever radio station I found; was playing this bloody record just to annoy me.

Despite the uncertainty of any diagnosis at that time, there was never any explanation of their investigations, no talk of what my illness might be. The days seemed never-ending and arduous, friendless, sad, perplexing, and uncomfortable, and quite often I wondered if I was just becoming paranoid.

Where was fate taking me? The small fragment of optimism was replaced by despondency, as I lay trapped in this hospital bed, the marching sound of mystery footsteps passing by without a word being spoken. There was a cascade of voices down the corridor, too far away to hear what they were saying, but loud enough to understand that their laughter signified happiness.

Through the window of my internment, a large expanse of lush green lawn was occupied by a family of blackbirds. Unaware of my predicament, they searched the soil for worms. Beyond them, I could see the silent movement of traffic heading out of the town. All signs of life outside, that carried on as normal, whilst I felt all alone; my mind was unequivocally confused and frightened; unsure as to what was happening, unaware as to why I was feeling so terrible.

Between investigations and when time allowed, some nursing staff would make any excuse to drop into my cubicle and chat. As most of them were young, it was a welcome change to being alone, and the mundane routine of examinations during those long, painful and generally unhappy days.

My despair was exacerbated by the fear of all the different investigations that I had to endure. What did they mean, and what were they looking for? As I was given no answers or explanations, I couldn't help but wonder, what were they hiding?

The night sweats continued nightly. Naturally, the nurses were aware that this was a symptom of my condition, but as a naive and immature eighteen-year-old, I was terrified that they would think that I had wet the bed due to incontinence. Such a silly thought, really, but it's remarkable what goes through an adolescent's mind at such a difficult time.

It seemed that there was an almost constant tirade of prodding and poking here, there and everywhere, and I was perplexed at the nature of their search as explanations were not readily forthcoming. I suppose in many respects, one could argue that I should have asked. But in all honesty, I was prepared to let them get on with it in the hope that once a conclusion had been reached I would be the first to know.

However, this would be a wrong assumption on my part. In addition, I was not a very confident eighteen-year-old, therefore; I was content to let them get on with their search. There was the daily ritual of at least one doctor coming to see me with the very same questions that had been asked the day before.

Twice each week there would be an entourage of white coats dutifully following the consultant. All of whom, wanting to push me here and squeeze me there, listen to my chest and then look quizzically at the Consultant, turning to him for words of wisdom. Meanwhile, one of the swellings in my neck had been surgically removed; the lump, which was the size of a walnut, was excised under local anaesthetic, and then sent for microscopic examination.

The procedure, known as a biopsy, was a painless operation, but not all other procedures would prove so innocent or indeed painless. Later in the week, my bowels would be put through their paces in the search for a conclusion to my illness. The unpleasant and nauseating 'Barium Swallow' was a disgusting white concoction that tasted of, well, nothing I'd tasted before, and it certainly was not savoury I can assure you.

The barium is impermeable to X-rays and, therefore, it is used to highlight abnormalities in either the stomach or the bowel after a series of X-rays have been taken. My bowels were taken to the next level of investigation when once again the radiology department would seek new ways to explore the inner depths of my colon.

I was wheeled into the x-ray room unprepared for this next exploration, as I had been given no prior explanation of what was to take place. As I lay on my side, the radiographer told me of her intention, a plastic tube would be placed into my bottom and barium pumped in as if they were seeking to insulate my innards.

As I am sure you can imagine, it wasn't a very comfortable experience and I can certainly confirm that it was not enjoyable, but it didn't stop there. No sooner did the barium flow into my bowels like cavity wall insulation than the table, I was lying on, started to twist and turn like a fairground ride.

This spinning and turning would enable a new series of films to see my bowels from different angles. Following this invasion of my dignity, I was only too pleased to get back to my solitary confinement for some peace.

The next day, I was taken across to the newly built diagnostic centre located at South Tyneside General Hospital for what was supposed to be one of the most important investigations, which would not only rule out one diagnosis but help to confirm another. I was taken into a small cubicle where I was met by a man with a fancy title, the Consultant Oncologist, who explained that the procedure I was about to undergo was a bone marrow investigation!

It didn't sound too bad, or, was the Consultant just a good salesman? He went on to ask if I had any objections to the junior doctor doing the procedure. '*Of course not,*' I replied, after all, a doctor was a doctor, what difference could it make? Not for the first time, my assumption was wrong. The junior doctor had no problem placing the local anaesthetic into the skin around my breastbone, where the biopsy was to be taken from.

However, he struggled to get any kind of leverage onto the biopsy needle he was using, and that was supposed to extract a sample of the bone marrow from my delicate skeleton. In hindsight, he lacked the necessary experience to undertake the technique with competence, and his struggle was such that he climbed onto the investigation couch with me to force more pressure on the needle.

Yes, local anaesthetic had been used but, either there was insufficient of the dammed stuff in there or he had been a butcher in a previous life, alternatively, I was just a big softie. Seriously though, I was now struggling to tolerate the investigation and I think the Consultant realized this, and he took over the procedure and secured the required sample in a few minutes.

Thank goodness that was over; I felt my chest was about to collapse like wet tissue paper. Once again, without explanation, I was wheeled out and transported back to the Ingham Infirmary for a much-needed rest and a large helping of painkillers. A couple of days later and my parents were taken to one side and told the news that all parents fear. My diagnosis was a malignancy, cancer.

It appeared to be a disease called Hodgkin lymphoma, stage IV, and the outcome was far from favourable. Such was the extent of the disease that there was only a 50% chance of surviving, and that depended upon how I responded to the treatment. Failing to respond to treatment would diminish my chances of survival even further.

Lymphoid tissue malignancies are grouped, into one of two diseases, those being Hodgkin lymphoma and all other lymphomas referred to as Non-Hodgkin lymphomas. These are uncommon cancers of the lymphatic system and are of unknown cause; Hodgkin lymphoma is most common among fifteen to thirty-year-olds, with a higher incidence among males.

Thomas Hodgkin first described the disease way back in 1832.

Mam and Dad were told by a Consultant that he would have liked to have seen me much earlier. He was rather bemused as to why I had been put on Valium and not referred to the hospital. In addition to the Consultant's bewilderment at the delay and the strange prescription of antidepressants by my family doctor, what would astound me was that, according to Mam, the Consultant encouraged them not to tell me of the diagnosis.

It seemed that was something they did not need a lot of encouragement to agree to. That was wrong on so many levels, but the decision was taken with the best of intentions, and of course, at the time, I had no idea of the collusion being acted out. I understand why my Mam and Dad were happy to go along with this, as there is no worse sensation in the world than being told that your child has cancer, and they would have wanted to protect me, but that doesn't mean I agree with the sentiment.

So, it turned out that I was not told of my diagnosis. Therefore, denied the opportunity to be involved in the decision-making process and to have at least some small degree of control as to what was going to happen to me. That's a basic right for any adult; surely it wasn't too much to ask for?

That decision by proxy still causes me great concern even today. It was my opinion that neither the Consultant nor my parents had heard of the veracity principle, which highlights the ethical obligation, to tell the truth. Or the underlying principle of patient collaboration, which regards the patient as being capable of offering suggestions and being involved in the decision-making process. I was that patient, but my voice had been silenced.

After the diagnosis, my Dad visited his father to tell him of the devastating news, and he responded by informing him that he had money in the bank and that if it was needed. It could be used to search out the best treatment that would afford me the best opportunity of getting well. However, Dad did not take up this option, and he and my mam placed their trust in the local hospital and its dedicated staff.

Having decided to exclude me from my diagnosis, the greatest concern now for my parents was trying to keep this information from me. However, their immediate concern was the fact that there was another Hodgkin lymphoma patient on the same ward as me, and they did not want me anywhere near him, although unknown to them, it was too late.

I was undergoing all of these investigations to conclusively determine the cause of my symptoms, while Joe had already been diagnosed with Hodgkin lymphoma some five years earlier and was currently very poorly; he was terminally ill and sadly died during my stay in the ward. Only days before his death, I had sat with Joe, and although I wasn't aware of either his diagnosis or his terminal state, even to my untrained eye I could see he was not a well man.

My Mam in particular was especially concerned, in case, I discovered the cause of his illness, and I would not only be upset over his condition, but it could lead me to inadvertently discover my diagnosis, the diagnosis that was currently being hidden from me. This kind of problem occurs simply because of this type of collusion, although admittedly, they acted with the best of intentions, it was doomed to fail from the offset.

Furthermore, Mam and Dad had decided not to inform my younger sister, Allyson, about my diagnosis. Once again, the merits of this action can be debated, but, as Allyson was only thirteen years old, I could clearly understand their rationale for this move. It would be two years later before she realized that the condition was a cancer diagnosis.

Interestingly, Allyson would later confirm that she was pleased that she was not told, claiming that she would have struggled to come to terms with it. However, she could equally see things from my perspective, and how frustrated I was at being declined the information that I was entitled to in the first instance.

Rather strangely, it seemed that all of a sudden, very few of my friends wanted to visit me in hospital, and when I eventually got home, they were noticeable only by their absence. It transpired that Mam had bumped into my best friend, Robbo, on the local bus and had told him that I had cancer. She also informed him that I did not know my diagnosis, and her instructions were clear — under no circumstances should I be told!

So, it wasn't long before my friends were made aware of this stigmatizing diagnosis. I later found out that the reason they didn't visit was their fear of the word cancer and not knowing what on earth they could talk to me about. Perhaps they thought the look on their faces would give the game away, and they were worried about how I would react once I realized I had the frightening disease of cancer.

I can understand their fear, and I certainly do not hold any grudges towards them. Then again, perhaps it was their fear of my Mam! One of the biggest dilemmas with a cancer diagnosis is the fact that many sufferers do not look unwell. It is a master of disguise, a hidden poison, a denizen from the unknown. And so it was that many of my friends would ultimately say that very thing.

You do not look as though you have cancer. But what does a cancer patient look like? It is not a respecter of creed, colour, or social standing — everyone is at risk. Before starting the planned chemotherapy — I was transferred to Newcastle General Hospital for some additional tests, which would determine specific issues relating to the lymphoma.

It was then that I was admitted to a specialist ward for cancer patients, yet when I arrived at the ward and even though some men had already lost their hair, due to my ignorance and naivety, I did not realize that this ward was solely for cancer patients.

However, whilst in Newcastle General, I overheard one of the doctors discussing my case with another and just by pure chance happened to hear the diagnosis of Hodgkin lymphoma. Now, this meant nothing whatsoever to me and I didn't give it a second thought, not knowing that this was a threat to my very existence. Coincidentally, the following day, I bought a newspaper, and it seemed fate had then decided to take a hand and deliver an unexpected revelation.

One particular story in this tabloid would not only shock me, it caused me such heartache that my emotions erupted, my tears being followed by anger, and frustration. It brought a realization that the life unfolding in front of me may well be shorter than I had hoped. The story in question had a headline; 'A Crossroads Star Tells His Sad Secret.'

The character, a wheelchair-bound Sandy played by Richard Tonge in the soap opera 'Crossroads' had been hiding a grim secret from millions of fans,' he was fighting his battle against Hodgkin lymphoma. Now, this interested me, as I suddenly realized that this was the same condition the doctors said I had.

Frighteningly, the article went on to reveal that Hodgkin lymphoma was cancer!

I was completely taken aback, this cannot be right. My mind became numb, and my emotions were everywhere, but where they should be. I paused for breath and had to read the article again, but sure enough, it was a cancerous condition. Why did no one tell me?

My mind raced. My head was spinning with confusion, a kaleidoscope of emotional turbulence. I experienced a whirlwind of changing feelings. Nothing could have prepared me for such a shock, perhaps I had misheard, or the doctors had been talking about someone else! Except, deep down inside, I knew they had been discussing me.

I now knew my diagnosis, but I certainly didn't know what lay ahead and the battle I was about to undertake. Undoubtedly, this was a roller coaster ride, which I had never ridden before, and I wanted to get off quickly. One moment I was up, the next, I was on the bottom without any control over how to steer my life.

My breath shortened, and my heart pounded so loudly I was sure the patient in the next bed could hear it. Panic gripped me. Fear swirled through my mind, dragging me into despair — then, just as suddenly, an inexplicable euphoria. Moments later, I crashed into a tearful low so deep it felt like I was scraping the ground. A storm of emotions and questions followed.

Anger. How dare my GP say I was depressed? And how could my so-called friends abandon me when I needed them most?

Frustration. How was I supposed to cope with a life-threatening illness?

Hopelessness. Why even bother with treatment when this disease was a death sentence?

I didn't understand these emotions, let alone know how to manage them.

Betrayal. How could my parents keep this from me, treating me like a child?

Guilt. Was this my fault? The consequence of my life choices?

Fear. Would I even have a future?

Doom. As far as I knew, no one survived cancer.

Determination. I had so much to live for, and I wasn't ready to give up.

Gratitude. At least it was me and not my younger sister, Allyson.

I was drowning in a flood of emotions with no one to guide me, no one to help me make sense of it all. Tearful, and desperate, I forced myself to focus.

Somewhere in my mind, I needed to find a reason to keep going — some spark of inspiration to pull me through this nightmare.

In some respects, I had exactly that in the music of Hawkwind. However, there were times, many times when it was just impossible to control my emotions, times when my ability to focus was beyond my comprehension, and times when I would need more than music. Emotions so intense, that I struggled to grasp, or understand, the gravity of my predicament.

Mam was flabbergasted when she came into the hospital later that day to find that I knew about the diagnosis, my diagnosis. She had come to visit with my Dad and a couple of relatives. I wanted answers but didn't get any, but I felt this was not the time to argue. In addition, and paradoxically, I could understand what they did, and why they did it, even so, that still didn't make it right.

More importantly, I honestly didn't feel as if I had any fight in me, or what little I had — I was going to need it for the long, gruelling battle that lay ahead.

'*How did you think you were going to hide this cancer from me?*' I asked through gritted teeth.

Hurt and tearful, Mam cried, and I could see that Dad was close to tears as well. It led me to feel guilty for being so abrupt. They felt my pain during the months of illness and tried to diminish it by protecting me from the diagnosis.

A diagnosis of cancer brings with it an alteration to every aspect, universally to your life. Your thoughts divert off at tangents during the most inopportune moments and serve as a constant reminder that cancer is a life-threatening disease. A convergence of negative and positive emotions would cause regular emissions of confusion and bewilderment.

Before discharge from ward 38, another blood transfusion was arranged as I was found to be anaemic once again due to the aggressive nature of the predatory cancer now stalking my body. On the day of discharge, I was started on a course of steroids, Prednisolone 10 mg three times daily, and also a drug called Procarbazine, 50 mg three times daily.

The ultimate plan was chemotherapy, but with so many drugs available, the right combination had to be carefully selected. The medical team needed more information to determine the most effective treatment — one that would give me the best chance of overcoming this aggressive disease. In the meantime, the two drugs I had started would at least begin to take effect.

Although not being aware of it yet, I would develop a crucially important relationship with Ward 38 at Newcastle General Hospital, but that would be many years in the future. It would not only be instrumental in my illness, but it would also be significantly influential in my future years, fate being the governing factor.

Two days later, I woke to find my body covered in a furious, unexplained rash. The itching was unbearable — I wanted to scratch until my skin was raw. Alarmed, Mam contacted the hospital, and I was readmitted to the Ingham Infirmary for further investigation. Though I felt unwell, it wasn't noticeably worse than the night before — except now, my skin felt like it was on fire.

Despite this, and an absence of other typical symptoms, the medical staff thought that this may well have been meningitis, and I was, therefore, isolated and had the usual barrage of blood tests. It turned out not to be meningitis, it was a simple reaction to the Procarbazine, and after stopping the drug it settled down after twenty-four hours of the appropriate treatment. Once again, I was on my way home.

Chapter 4
A Kaleidoscope of Emotion

The proposed treatment for this lymphoma was the dreaded chemotherapy, which was due to start the following Thursday as an outpatient at South Tyneside District General Hospital. Everyone has heard of chemotherapy treatment, hair loss, lethargy, vomiting and eventually, you die, that was my fear. That was my ignorant perception.

In the days leading up to Thursday's appointment, my mind was filled with thoughts of this terrible treatment that I was about to receive. Despite being admittedly immature, I wasn't completely stupid; I had seen television programmes about people with cancer, and had seen the torture, and torment they went through with this treatment, and that terrified me.

On Thursday, I attended the outpatient department, and almost immediately I was taken into a cubicle. But, not just any cubicle though, it was the same cubicle where the torturous bone marrow persecution had been carried out only a week earlier. The Consultant came in and passed the usual pleasantries and, I think in hindsight, his distraction therapy was perfect as I gave very little thought to the tray of large injections that lay only inches away from me.

He lifted the needle that he intended to place in my forearm, ready for the delivery of the proposed drugs, and before I knew it, he had access to my veins. It is quite strange the things our minds allow us to remember and forget, but it is with crystal clear clarity that I can still see that very first injection. A slow motion movement, toward my arm. The rapid beat of my heart accompanied by its rising volume — a clear indication that my fear was higher than any time previously and unsure as to how my deteriorating body would react to this toxic poison being pumped into it.

The chemotherapy drugs flowed uneventfully into my veins, rating a zero on the scale of excitement. My initial thought was that this chemotherapy was a bit of a breeze, not the terrible treatment I had imagined at all, or was I being too optimistic? Irrespective, my main thought was, would it be able to stop this cancer? That was the million-dollar question, and no one could answer that question, even though I never asked it.

I do believe that much of the fear and stigma relating to cancer treatments must be laid at the door of the media. How sad it is, when they could have an educative effect on the public, they all too often tend to sensationalize cancer and its necessary treatments. It's a great shame when someone comes along and is given a cancer diagnosis and told they need to have chemotherapy, then feel psychologically destroyed having previously read an article in a tabloid that portrayed the event so negatively.

I am not saying that cancer and its uncertain treatment are easy to get through or that it is not a serious issue; of course, it is. I just feel strongly that many, although not all, of the media, fail to report cancer facts accurately. All too typically, there is a sense of melodrama because it will sell newspapers or is good television.

That cannot be right if it is distorted to such a degree that it gives an incorrect perception to those undergoing or about to undertake treatment for a cancer diagnosis. The media have a responsibility to report matters precisely and without prejudice.

The drug regimen I was going to receive was called 'MOPP,' an acronym for the drugs to be administered.

The plan was to have six cycles of this treatment and each would be given at three weekly intervals, an important fact to remember! There had, in hindsight, been no formal or even informal consent for this treatment that was planned. Neither had there been any explanation of what I was to expect after the chemotherapy had been administered.

This, in my view, is one of the most significant reasons why such stigma is attached to cancer treatments; a simple explanation of the potential side effects is vital and can allay so much fear from a patient's perspective. What's more, providing patient's with written information is a vital component of the empowerment process.

The drugs had been administered and the needle removed. That was my first chemotherapy treatment now behind me and I planned to make my way home. At the time, my grandfather lived just over the road from the hospital, and he was aware of my diagnosis, and had told my Dad that if I felt up to it, I should call in after the inaugural treatment.

I didn't need a second asking, as my grandfather, William Slater Pattison, was a veteran of the First World War; he had been a prisoner of war, incarcerated in Döberitz, near Berlin. He had some incredible stories to tell and I loved hearing them. Therefore, after my first treatment I called in to see him for a short while, after all, my war had just started.

After a brief visit, I headed home, only ten minutes away by taxi. At home, mam had prepared one of her famous homemade mince pies. Of course, the steroids I was taking at the time ensured my appetite was voracious and when she asked, '*How much of the pie do you want?*' I replied, '*All of it.*' The pie was devoured in a matter of minutes.

Everything was going so well, I could not understand the negativity that went hand in hand with chemotherapy. This treatment had been pretty straightforward, and not what I had expected, or did my optimistic anticipation come too soon?

No more than twenty minutes later, my stomach began to gurgle and churn and then, to say that I was sick is perhaps the biggest understatement so far. I experienced projectile vomit from deep down within, and I felt that my stomach had been turned inside out. In addition, it was not just a matter of being sick and emptying the contents of my stomach — as the retching continued for hours, which then stretched into many days.

During the night, the nausea was unbearable, the moment I got out of bed to visit the toilet, the very act of moving caused repetitive retching, which by this time yielded nothing but bile and brash, which lasted for over a week. Unable to eat, fearing the sickness, my resolve was just about destroyed; I had never imagined anything like this, and I could not believe that anyone could feel this way.

Disillusioned, feeling tortured and persecuted like never before, my greatest fear was the fact that I would be unable to face more of this mental and physical torment. Yet, tearfully, knew that I would have no choice and this was just the beginning.

A week after my first chemotherapy, and I was back in the hospital, but not because of persistent nausea and vomiting. I awoke one morning to find that I had the biggest lips that cosmetic surgery could buy.

It was yet another allergic reaction to one of the drugs I had taken and again, the Procarbazine was implicated. It seemed strange to me that the drug I had reacted to previously had been given to me again. However, the Procarbazine was a vital ingredient of the treatment regimen and, therefore, they had decided to re-challenge my body with it.

This treatment was so unforgiving, was there anything it would not do to your body systems? Fortunately, after ant-histamine treatment, just a few days later, those rubber lips had disappeared. I was no longer controlling my body. It was being manipulated by the chemotherapy, leaving me like a drug-fuelled robot, an alien being with my actions controlled by the toxic drugs.

Chemotherapy treatment was repeated every twenty-one days, yet of those days, only ten were absent of the horrid side effects. Thankfully and without exception, my friends soon began to visit again. That is, once they knew that I was aware of my diagnosis. And they were aware that others had not fallen into the vast chasm of silence, and the fear of saying the wrong thing to their friend with the big 'C.'

My friends were very supportive and indeed protective. Later, in months to come, when I would eventually feel strong enough to get out and socialize, the lads, almost without exception, would demonstrate big brother protection. If I was pushed the wrong way, even innocently, then there was always someone there to ensure that it was accidental, and I was safe.

I very much appreciated this protection, feeling very fragile but also at times a little like royalty. Significantly, there were never any incidences of actual fights or other trouble, and I knew that there was always a careful eye focused on me.

It was almost three weeks from the delivery of my first treatment, but to my disgust and sadness; I awoke one morning to find clumps of hair on my pillow.

The cruelty of this chemotherapy knew no bounds; a tear rolled down my cheek to remind me of my mental instability. With anger in my heart, I decided to get my hair cut. It was pointless having long black locks that were certain to drop out as more, and more of the dammed poison was pumped into my veins. I found this a particularly hard concept to accept.

My hair was an important part of my identity, my persona. Even my identity, as I saw it, was being eroded. My parents never commented on my hair, either as it started to fall out or when I got it cut short, as they just knew how significant it had been to me. At a later time, I would destroy every photograph of myself during that difficult time. Something I would regret in future years.

Naturally, I was feeling quite low at that time, and I required a sickness note for work, which meant a visit to my family doctor. I felt strongly that I would not see that imbecile that had the nerve, and guile, to discuss something he knew nothing about. The man who claimed that I was depressed, and then redirected his diagnosis to one of appendicitis. Instead, I asked to see the other doctor in the practice. However, I was just as taken aback when I went in to see her.

She looked me in the eyes having signed my sick note, and said, '*Have they told you your diagnosis?* Before I had a chance to reply, she blurted out, '*You have Leukaemia.*'

Mouth open aghast, you could have knocked me over with a feather. I snatched the sick note from her hand, told her that she was mistaken, and stormed out of her surgery without looking back. At home, I explained to my Mam what had been said, and she was so enraged that she rang the practice demanding to speak with the doctor.

Luckily for the doctor, she had gone out on a house call, which was probably just as well because Mam would certainly not have held anything back in her reprimand of the doctor's insensitive behaviour. Mam did speak with the receptionist, and told her exactly what she thought of the doctor's lack of communication skills. So I am sure it would have got back to the doctor.

One of the most important lessons my sister and I learned early in life was that you do not answer my mother back.

Days before my next chemotherapy treatment was due again, I began to feel physically sick. I knew exactly what I was about to experience, sickness and vomiting, twisted bowels and an inability to eat food for days, although it was not so much an inability to eat food, more of a fear of eating, as it was obvious what the consequence would be.

Apart from that, well, it was a breeze, nothing to it! But if only that were true, if only this were a bad dream and I could awaken from my nightmare. I could never have imagined that this foreign substance deep within my veins could cause such devastating effects; effects I'd never even dreamed about in my worst nightmare. A storm of unforgiving proportions.

The day finally came when I was to attend the day unit at South Tyneside District Hospital for my next chemotherapy treatment. I got there in plenty of time, and had my blood taken, and made my way around to the yellow waiting area, and at first, I was saddened at what I saw — so many old folk, whom I assumed were there for the same reason as me.

Not saddened at the sight of the old people, but at the thought of these people who had worked all of their lives and enjoyed what life had to offer, only to be blighted by this terrible affliction that is cancer. Yet, here we all were without much control over this feared disease, irrespective of age, amalgamated by the same bond.

Such negative thoughts made me think of my mortality, and whether I would be around for the next Hawkwind tour, and if I were, would I be well enough to sit through a concert without feeling sick? In the background, a voice shouted my name, and it was my turn to see the Consultant for my treatment.

I sluggishly dragged my feet into the consulting room to be faced by Dr Sheppard, who was a pleasant enough chap; it was just that I didn't feel very much like being pleasant, knowing what I was there for. He reminded me of Jerry Lewis in the starring role of the film, '*The Nutty Professor*,' dressed in his long white coat, his glasses perched on the end of his nose as he peered over the top of them at me. He had a slight overbite and frowned as he stood alongside me, as I lay on the couch. His feet clad in open-toed sandals.

Following a brief chat, he would twist his face up, just as the '*Nutty Professor*' did in the film. Then following a physical examination, he told me that my blood is satisfactory, the lumps in my neck, and under my arms have started to go down, and that the next treatment would be going ahead as planned.

Then, although the words stick in the back of my throat, I bravely ask the question that I was dreading the answer to, '*Am I going to get better from this*?'

Now, I cannot remember his exact words; actually, I don't think I recall any of his words, only the interpretation. I think looking back; his answer was what is commonly referred to as spin, also called deflection. What I do remember is that I was none the wiser following his response. But then perhaps I wanted to avoid knowing, and I decided to allow fate to take its course, thinking that what I didn't know couldn't hurt me. Therefore, I did not pursue it any further.

Before I knew it, the cold steel needle was in the back of my hand, and ready for the delivery of the toxic drugs. Three of the drugs were given this way, the first was an anti-sickness injection. I was of course, completely bewildered as to why it was called an anti-sickness drug because it was about as much use as my family doctor, and we know how good he was.

The second was a large volume of fluid which was called Nitrogen Mustard and was responsible for nausea and vomiting. The third drug called Vincristine and had the weirdest taste and smell sensation as it was being administered, a foul unpleasant metallic taste and a bizarre irritation to my nasal passage.

There did not appear to be any of my body systems that were not being affected, attacked or destroyed by this treatment. I felt that I was being systematically and unceremoniously ravaged.

During subsequent injections, I would ask for a large glass of orange to sip very slowly while the Vincristine was being given and although it did not eliminate the taste, it did help. Defencelessly I watched the drugs seep into my veins, my heart raced, my emotions bubbled to the surface and I felt tearful.

I was anticipating the violent sickness that I knew lay in wait. I feared more unknowns and, of course, something I believe is typical of all cancer patients, the uncertainty of what lay ahead in my future. The ultimate question spinning around my head, did I have a future? After completing the chemotherapy for the second time, I headed home feeling unsure about how and, indeed, if I wanted to continue with this ruthless treatment.

At this particular moment, however, I felt that I had no other option than to continue, at least for the moment. That was something that would plague me on and off for many months, causing inner conflict and self-confrontation. I decided not to call into my grandfather's this time as I felt it would be better not to start feeling sick in his house, after all, he was in his late seventies and that would have been unfair.

Once at home, I decided to eat only a light snack, as the large portion of mince pie had been the trigger following my first treatment. The doctor had changed the anti-sickness medication this time, so I was hopeful that I did not suffer as I did with my first treatment, fingers crossed. Sadly, within a couple of hours, I knew what was to follow, even though I had only experienced it once previously, there was no mistaking that feeling.

Following the predatory attack of the chemotherapy on my body, my stomach was preparing to erupt like an active volcano, waiting spontaneously to spew its contents once again. Sure enough, there was a crescendo of nausea followed by the sickness, and my stomach was soon aching as it had three weeks earlier. All I could do was retire to my bedroom, close the curtains and play some Hawkwind music.

Whilst it probably sounds silly to most people, it gave me a sense of escapism and, I suppose most importantly, distraction as I lay on my bed, confined by a chemical straitjacket with no escape. Irrespective of your situation, I believe everyone needs inspiration and motivation, but Hawkwind was far more than simple inspiration at that time; they are, as many will testify, a way of life, to love them is to be part of them, to enjoy a romantic affair with creation, invention and space rock.

Weeks later, I was naturally pleased to read that the band planned to tour later in the year, and this gave my deflated persona some much-needed inspiration. More importantly, as part of the tour, they were due to headline at the now-famous Reading rock festival. I intended to be part of that experience, to soak up the atmosphere, a free spirit destined to be part of the Hawkwind experience, and the thought of this was a great driving force for me.

I was struggling to come to terms with this evil cancer and, at times, my mind was constantly buzzing, fearing the impending and indiscriminate attack of the chemotherapy. Of course, I knew there was no point in adding to my woes by worrying, but that was easier said than done, as I could quite simply not control the strange and fearsome thoughts lingering in the canyons of my mind.

Occasionally, I felt ashamed at the way I was feeling sorry for myself, and there were times when I wanted to give myself a good kicking to try to pull myself together. I knew deep down, despite being an immature eighteen-year-old, that I had to stay focused and positive. In addition, I felt I was being unfair to my very supportive family by being so negative.

I had unconsciously decided early on in my journey that I would not share my innermost secrets, my fears and my depressive thoughts with my family. They were indeed suffering the same as me, and I wanted to avoid adding to their burden. Family life continued and seldom was there any discussion about cancer or treatments.

I would always undertake hospital visits alone, unaccompanied by choice, and that was a huge mistake! Between treatments, I had family and friends visit on regular occasions, but more often than not I simply could not be bothered by visitors, but I felt obligated to make trivial conversation.

Not only that, my friends, in particular, were always talking about their nights out, what they had been up to and, of course, the sticky scrapes they had got themselves into. I felt more depressed after their visits as I was becoming aware of what I was missing out on, the excitement, and mischief of adolescence, including girlfriends.

At other times, this talk just fuelled my motivation to try to beat this horrendous illness. It was a lonely time when isolation played weird mind games with my psychological status. But importantly, I found this a time of personal reflection and self-assessment to take stock and appreciate life itself. A time when I was thinking about things that I'd never considered previously.

I acknowledged that life is made up of uncomplicated, but beautiful things which we often do not appreciate. Life is a tapestry of simple, marvellous moments that typically go unnoticed. The countless glistening stars, floating effortlessly in the unlimited darkness of space, remind us of the universe's vastness — a wonder only equalled by the infinite grains of sand on a sunlit beach. The hypnotic rhythm of waves, tirelessly massaging the unprotected shoreline, which carries a timeless melody of peace. Marshmallow clouds drift lazily across the skyline, while birds soar gracefully on invisible thermals, embodying freedom and grace. And then there's the soothing rhythm of raindrops tapping gently against the window, a lullaby as you lie in bed, cocooned in thought.

Louis Armstrong captured it perfectly when he sang, '*And I think to myself, what a wonderful world.*'

After we are born, the only certain fact in life is that one day we will die; the only variance for us is when and how. Typically, it is only after some life-changing experience that we consciously reflect on life generally and appreciate its significance, its sanctity, its beauty, and of course, its uniqueness.

How many of us have ever taken time to sit and admire the everyday world, just simple things like the wind rustling through the creaking branches of an ancient oak tree? Then, of course, there is nothing more impressive than the first snow flurry of winter, taking a handful of virgin snow and feeling each of your fingers tingle with numbness.

What a fantastic world this is, and yet we know so little about life itself. There is so much to admire and respect about life and its uniqueness but, sadly, there are so many things in life to fear, including illness. But ultimately, what is the meaning of life? No one has that answer and, perhaps, no one ever will. What I do know is that confronting your mortality has a strange way of raising many intriguing issues, allowing you to see life from a different perspective.

A cancer diagnosis also elicits the bereavement process, grief, and feelings of loss are not just reserved for those individuals who have lost loved ones. Following a diagnosis of cancer, one goes through a multitude of recognized emotions; Denial, this can't be happening to me, it's a dream; Anger, why me, I've never done anything to deserve this; Bargaining, I will live my life respectably and go to church if only I'm well again; Depression, something I would become accustomed too; Acceptance, if this is my time, then I have to deal with it.

Of course, many people go through these emotions in many different ways and not necessarily in this order, and many of the emotions are revisited too. But at this particular juncture in my young existence, I felt as though I matured rapidly, appreciating that life, indeed, is a beautiful thing.

At times, staying positive and looking toward the future felt almost effortless. But in other moments, doubt crept in, making me feel weak for allowing negativity to take hold. I was painfully aware of my frail body — a shadow of what it once was. At just seven stone, I knew I needed to regain weight, not just for strength but for survival.

Monitoring my weight every day became an obsession, yet the pounds proved extremely difficult to gain as I continued to feel fatigued, and nauseated, and since food lacked taste, the task of gaining weight would prove hard in the short term. It was a vicious circle, and for that moment, a no-win situation.

Hope is so important; it is a skill that you must hone and cultivate — if you have hope, anything is possible. But, my lonely thoughts persecuted my optimism and removed my hope, thoughts so dark and negative they created my tears, and invaded every recess of my mind, and I struggled to battle those demons.

I considered life as a whole host of small islands of happiness surrounded by a deep sea of shit. You get onto one island and enjoy the happiness it has to offer, but all too often the tide swamps the island. You are once again left in the sea of shit until you can drag yourself onto the next island, this epitomized my life.

When it was time to go back to the hospital for further treatment, my mind was twisted, and full of fear, and indignation. No matter how hard I tried, I just could not escape the negative thoughts in the back of my mind. Entering the hospital, my body felt like a lonely, trembling leaf on the branch of a massive tree waiting for the first autumnal breeze to take control of it and whisk it away to who knows where?

Concerned and anxious about the impending treatment, I attended the blood room and had the requisite samples taken before heading round to the yellow waiting area that I was now familiar with. Waiting for the results only compounded the anxiety and fear, as they would dictate whether treatment would go ahead or not.

The nurse shouted my name and as it reverberated, bouncing menacingly off every wall, I reluctantly rose from my chair and trudged into the consulting room, struggling to hold back my delicate emotions.

'*Your blood is all fine to continue the next treatment*,' I'm told.

However, just before the chemotherapy is given there is the inconvenience of the physical examination, and as I was laid on the examination couch I knew that I was close to tears. Anger, and uncontrollable panic set in, and even though it was still early days in my cancer journey, I knew that feeling, the anguish, and the doubt in my resolve. I knew I was beginning to falter as the chemotherapy was brought into the room.

My frail body lay uncomfortably on the couch as the nurse provided me with a large glass of orange juice to take away that horrible metallic taste and the uncanny smell, created by the Vincristine as it was administered.

The Consultant smiled and said, '*Make a fist for me.*'

With my fist clenched, and my eyes closed, he slipped a needle into the back of my hand then reached for the first of the drugs, and in it went without resistance. Unexpectedly, my mind anticipated, and my stomach began to object. The brash welled up in my mouth, and then I just knew I was going to vomit.

No matter how I tried to control it, I heaved into the receptacle held by the compassionate nurse. Tears now rolled down my cheeks, not just due to embarrassment, but also sheer fear, and concern at the impending side effects I knew were lurking just around the corner. Dr Sheppard had no option but to abandon the remaining treatment, and I was admitted to the day ward, awaiting a bed in one of the wards.

A cancer diagnosis is like a stormy sea, the scariest tempest imaginable which batters your body, subsequently, you have to learn to navigate through the storm if you want to survive. As I lay on the bed, I was conscious of the footsteps walking around outside. The occasional laughter of the nurses discussing their recent escapades, yet although they were only a few feet away, I felt as if I was a million miles away from everyone, abandoned by society.

Unwanted, and uninvited thoughts wandered through my mind — I knew there was no benefit submitting to the darkness that consumed my mind and steered me in a direction of self-destruction, but, I struggled to fight it.

Eventually, I was subsequently transferred to Newcastle General Hospital, where I would remain until my treatment was completed and the anti-sickness medication could be reviewed. When I arrived at Ward 38, Newcastle General Hospital, I was greeted by a nurse, and shown to my bed.

Later, a young doctor arrived, his presence signalling yet another round of prodding, poking, and the same set of questions I had answered countless times before. His voice was polite, professional, yet detached, as if I were just another case on his list. The monotony of it all frustrated me, but I lacked the energy to argue. I simply let the routine play out, staring past him at the ceiling, tracing the cracks with my eyes as if they held some hidden meaning.

Before the dreaded treatment could begin again, a nurse hooked me up to a drip containing the highest dose of Metoclopramide (anti-sickness) they could administer. The cold fluid seeped into my veins, sending a slow chill up my arm, making my fingers tingle slightly. The idea was to prevent the sickness before it started — an optimistic theory, but given my track record, I wasn't holding my breath. My body had become a battlefield, and I had little faith in reinforcements arriving in time.

Of all the chemotherapy drugs, Nitrogen Mustard (Mustine) was the most ruthless in its ability to induce violent sickness. The mere thought of it made my stomach twist. My nausea had already been unbearable, so the decision was made to swap it for Cyclophosphamide, a supposed lesser evil. I wasn't sure if that was a blessing or just another variation of the same torment.

At some point, exhaustion dragged me under, the anti-sickness drip working its temporary magic. The light dimmed, the beeping of machines fading into a dull rhythm, and I fell asleep. When I finally surfaced, my body felt heavy, limbs weighted down as though I had been sinking in deep water. My eyelids fluttered open to find a nurse and doctor standing at the foot of my bed, their gloved hands poised, ready to administer what I feared — more chemotherapy.

A flutter of nervous energy rippled through my stomach, but oddly, I felt calm. Perhaps it was the haze of sleep, numbing my anxiety before it could fully take hold. Perhaps I had simply resigned myself to the inevitable. Either way, as the toxic chemicals loomed closer; I took a deep breath and let it happen.

I asked for the orange drink before they started, and they both looked at me with bewilderment, I'm sure they thought I was crazy. However, there was no way they were starting that treatment without that orange, of that I was certain, and more importantly, it was neither of those two who had to endure the bizarre, and filthy taste of the Vincristine.

After the treatment, I tried sleeping but to no avail, and decided to walk along to the day room with my drip.

One of the guys, Tom, greeted me and asked what I was having, '*I think it's called COPP.*' I replied, '*Similar to me,*' He said.

We immediately began to compare notes, and it turned out that he also had Hodgkin lymphoma. He was in his early thirties, and was a policeman in Cumbria. He told me that his wife had left him recently as she couldn't cope with his cancer diagnosis — and I thought that I had problems. Tom and I struck up a good friendship over the coming months.

I clearly remember his optimism at the treatment he was receiving, and I recall being rather envious of his positive mental attitude, despite experiencing the same side effects as myself. Later in the evening, having attempted some food, my stomach began to gurgle, churn and then erupt as its entire contents were deposited into a large vomit bowl. So much for the anti-sickness infusion!

The next plan then was to try a drug called Lorazepam. The mode of action of this medication would not only sedate me, it also had an amnesic effect.

Have you ever tried sleeping in a hospital? Don't get me wrong, I'm not being ageist, but some old men could not half snore. If there were a category for snoring in the Olympic Games, I could have nominated a few of those guys, and there would be a good chance one of them would walk away with a gold medal.

At first, it was quite funny, the musical chorus of midnight snoring, but then it became annoying and frustrating as my sleep was not happening, unfortunately not a great deal can be done about the noise problem. There were private cubicles on the ward, but these were reserved for the more poorly patients, especially those who were dying. That very situation occurred one night during my stay in Ward 38.

The ward was busier than ever before, and the nursing staff appeared to be running around without pause and spending an awful lot of time around the old man's bed directly opposite to me. The curtains were secretively drawn around his bed and the light switched on. The remainder of the ward was in relative darkness as one doctor followed another doctor behind those curtains, and when one nurse went behind the curtains she was soon followed by another.

Then, the light was switched off and the doctors and nurses made their way from the curtains but, significantly, left the curtains closed. Some while later, I was awoken by one of the nurse's closing my curtains, having just closed those adjacent to me. Five minutes afterwards, and our curtains were drawn back, and there before me was an empty bed — freshly made linen neatly folded, and no sign of the little old man who had been the scene of such activity only an hour earlier.

Sadly, he had passed away, yet another victim of the unforgiving, and ruthless cancer. My eyes filled with tears when I realized what had happened, and a silent acknowledgement that this cancer was quite capable of claiming me as well.

Many a night in the hospital would be spent in the dayroom, often with the night staff, and I do believe it is important to highlight that I had nothing but admiration and praise for these nurses. What they had to cope with was not the most pleasant job in the world, but still, their dedication and uncomplaining approach impressed me immensely.

Interestingly, I had noticed that several patients on the ward were not having chemotherapy, they were having a different treatment for their cancer and it was called radiotherapy. It seemed to my inexperienced eye that this was a far easier treatment option than the chemotherapy that my body was struggling to accept. Why was that not given to me?

I thought I would make the appropriate investigations on this one and perhaps get the treatment changed, as that would be so much easier, and then perhaps I could get back to work and also the forthcoming Hawkwind tour. So, my mind was made up, I want radiotherapy. But, how wrong could I be?

Another fellow patient was Steve. He had a different type of lymphoma from me, but he was still going through the dreaded chemotherapy, and that made us kindred spirits. In addition, he was about my age and, therefore, we had much in common. Steve was about to finish his chemotherapy and start radiotherapy.

Unknown to me at the time, Steve had an aggressive, advancing disease that required radiotherapy in addition to chemotherapy. This demonstrated that these lymphomas were not only unpredictable but also indiscriminate and predatory. The Consultant came around later that Friday morning and decided that he wanted to keep me in for observation and monitoring until Monday.

However, he did not mention my request for radiotherapy that I had earlier submitted via the nursing staff and as he left, I felt betrayed, let down, disappointed and dejected. The nurse in question told me that she had mentioned my request to Dr Sheppard, but he dismissed it out of hand as a viable option. Surely, an explanation of his rationale might have been in the spirit of good communication.

I suppose if I had one criticism of the medical and nursing fraternity back then, it was poor communication. As patients, we were aware that the majority of doctors and nurses were not prepared to confront or even discuss the patient's questions and fears regarding cancer. Peer support at that time was invaluable, and I believe it is equally important today.

Patients essentially need each other as support. Yes, of course, we could not do without the medical, and nursing staff. However, doctors and nurses go off shift and can forget about work until they are next on duty. Cancer patients cannot do that, seven days a week, twenty-four hours every day. As a cancer patient, you are on duty permanently with malignancy as your main accomplice.

Often, I and others would be up most of the night. We would discuss our mutual concerns about the uncertainty of our future — comparing experiences regarding different investigations, and treatments. That support was, and remains, an invaluable resource. And, what about when you are discharged, out of the hospital, and back at home, then there becomes a sense of isolation as that mutual peer support is lost until your next admission?

Needless to say, family members are essential; they do everything they can, and most often a lot more. However, they quite simply are not in the same situation as you and therefore, the mutual support patients offer each other is priceless.

By Saturday morning I was feeling much better, something was having the desired effect.

Tom had suggested that we took a walk outside to get the morning paper from a local shop, rather than wait for them to appear on the ward. This we did, and as we headed back to the hospital, Tom suggested that we stop, and have a drink in the public house next to the hospital. This seemed like a reasonable idea to me, and so we did exactly that.

The pub was empty, and we sat with a pint of beer passing polite conversation but, as our glasses emptied, it seemed that both at the same time we turned and faced each other. Our faces became ever more flushed with redness, and we just knew something strange was happening. Therefore, we returned quickly back to the hospital, and onto the ward, only to be greeted by the Sister who took one look at us and smirked.

'*I know where you two have been!*' she exclaimed.

We felt like a couple of young schoolchildren having been scolded by the headmistress. The drug Procarbazine is an oral capsule, and forms a significant part of the treatment, as it is taken for seven days.

However, unknown to Tom and me, it interacts with many products, including alcohol which causes the facial flushing that we had experienced, and although there was no major problem other than this flushing, and the fact that alcohol would have a greater effect than normal — we did feel like a pair of idiots.

This, the third cycle of treatment, was certainly not as bad as the first two.

Was this because I was kept in hospital or due to the change to the anti-sickness medication or the fact that I was having treatment at the same time as others, and had some serious peer support?

On Monday, I headed back home feeling much more positive than ever before. When I got home, Mam was in the kitchen, and when I wandered in there she just smiled at me, and looked down at the floor. There in front of me was a delightful little puppy, a cross Labrador/German Sheppard, and she was a real beauty.

Sheba, as she would be named, would be my new companion, a distraction from the thought, and worry of cancer, and its impending treatment. Unknown to me, Mam had made the long travel of approximately fifty miles by public transport, just to buy this puppy for me. The background nausea was still present, and this would remain with me for days to follow, but Sheba was a good companion and a great distraction.

The future treatments had been planned as an inpatient at Newcastle, and this pleased me greatly as it allowed me ongoing contact with Tom, and the other patients in the same position as me. The mutual support that went hand in hand with that contact was essential, support that only another cancer patient could provide.

Chapter 5
Bury My Heart at Wounded Knee

Until recently, chemotherapy was one of the primary treatments for cancer, but its indiscriminate nature poses significant challenges for patients. The objective of chemotherapy is to destroy cancer cells. However, it also damages healthy cells, particularly those that are vital for immunity, leaving patients susceptible to infections. And, infections can be life-threatening. That vulnerability can lead to complications that will only add to the already gruelling experience.

It was during one of my periods of chemotherapy that I picked up an infection and a large boil developed on the left side of my cheek. As my white cell count was low — rather than receding with antibiotics, the boil was getting bigger, and angrier, and more painful.

Mam was a great believer in the good old-fashioned remedies, such as the bread poultice. This hot and painful concoction was applied to the offending boil, but despite this natural intervention, it made little improvement. On my return to the hospital, the doctor decided it required lancing (cut with a surgical blade).

This was not a pleasant experience and even today there remains a small scar where the boil demonstrated just how unforgiving chemotherapy treatment can be. Despite my previous inability to cope with treatment, rather ironically, I now found myself desperate to get on with the chemotherapy. My mental anguish aside, the assault and battery on my body; I recognized that the sooner I could get the treatment behind me, the sooner I would be able to move my life forward.

Unfortunately, on this occasion, due to the persistence of the unsightly boil, I had to wait longer for the privilege of my next chemical torture. It was felt that because of the infection and the low white cell count, my treatment should be delayed for a further week. While this decision made complete sense, this delay would also serve to prolong my usual pre-treatment anxiety and extend my mental persecution.

Living with cancer delivers many challenges almost every day, and these challenges can often be unexpected. This massive boil on the side of my face was certainly unexpected. It caused me a great deal of distress, pain, and psychological despair. The simple fact is that you do not earn respect from cancer as a disease; the truth is that it simply fails to respect you as an individual. It is the ultimate of challenges, both physically and mentally.

My mood was once again at a particularly low ebb, my mind was obsessed, and confused by the fact that I required more chemotherapy, but uneasy that I had to wait for it. Soon, I would make my own treatment decision, but not necessarily the right one. My life was being acted out in a maze, at every turn, an obstacle held back what little optimism I had, and I questioned whether I had the strength to negotiate more obstacles.

But, only days later, my negative mood changed as I was taken by surprise when I opened the front door to greet the postman holding a large package addressed to me, Mr John Pattison Junior. I signed for the parcel and rushed inside to find that the parcel was sent from Aunty Mary, and Uncle Jerry in North Carolina. They had sent me some authentic Indian wear, including a couple of headbands, neck beads, books, a waistcoat, and a special wallet.

On each piece, there was a ticket demonstrating that this was indeed authentic. Hand made by the Cherokee residents of Oconaluftee Village in the Great Smokey Mountains of North Carolina. Mam had been writing to her sister in America to keep her informed of my condition and treatment; at the same time, she had quite innocently mentioned my interest in Native American culture.

My Mam's youngest sister Mary had married an American GI after the war, and subsequently immigrated to America. Needless to say, I had plenty of time on my hands at present, and reading would prove a simple way to pass the time; I opened the cover of 'Bury My Heart at Wounded Knee' by Dee Brown.

It gave a fascinating insight into the many facets of the native cultures but also told of the exploitation, and persecution of the Native Americans and, once started, I found it difficult to put it down. I had only read a few chapters, and felt that one day I must visit these proud yet undermined people.

At that juncture in time, I did not realize the impact this book would have on my life, and what 'Wounded Knee' would mean to me in years to come. The inspiration I gleaned from those pages would prove motivational above and beyond Hawkwind. How exactly those brave, proud, and yet exploited people would unknowingly influence my life was, at this point, beyond my comprehension.

I wrote many letters to Aunty Mary, and many of these letters included my appreciation of Indian culture and spirituality. More importantly, my desire to visit America, and significantly the indigenous people who had been so wronged by history, was insatiable. Perhaps one day it would be possible. At present, I couldn't imagine that the impact of this book, and particularly the struggles of the Lakota people, part of the great Sioux Empire, would have such a bearing on what lay ahead, And my life generally.

Towards the end of July and just before the chemotherapy was due again, Hawkwind appeared at the Mayfair in Newcastle and I knew I had to be there.

Having finished *Bury My Heart at Wounded Knee,* I had a newfound focus and despite my ongoing malaise, I dragged myself to the show despite feeling thoroughly washed out and drained of enthusiasm.

It wasn't until I arrived at the Mayfair that I realized I would struggle to stay for the entire show, and all for good reason. Thanks to my ever-present companions, the dominant force of cancer fatigue, and the ever-present feeling of nausea, I tearfully made my way out of the hall and headed home.

My resentment of this disease was growing stronger and stronger as the weariness continued to impact my determination to try to enjoy what pleasures I could.

Worse was to follow, as much to my disgust, a chest infection followed close on the heels of the boil that had unceremoniously scarred my face. This infection forced me into hospital in August. I had no choice, but to abandon my plans to travel to Reading and the rock festival — headlined by Hawkwind.

My lonely persecution was intolerable. I felt isolated by a hidden disease, and attacked by its very consequences, my motivation was stolen.

To distract me from the disappointment of missing the Reading festival, I decided to read more about the Lakota Sioux. They were, after all, my new driving force, my absent guides, my inspiration to cope with an invisible illness, and most of all, I felt they could indirectly support my mental instability.

A few days after my discharge from South Shields hospital, the chest infection was now behind me. I made my way up to Newcastle for the fourth cycle of delayed chemotherapy; hoping that some of the guys that I had met on my last admission would also be there. Indeed, they were, and Tom and I met in the day room.

I was still bemused by the fact that some patients at Newcastle General Hospital were having radiotherapy treatment, and I was confused as to why it had not been offered to me. No one had taken the time to explain why I had not been considered for this treatment. Of course, there was a perfectly logical explanation, which I would learn about later.

With me on this admission was Hawkwind, they had recently brought out a new album called *Warrior on the Edge of Time.* Truly one of their great works, and I had it on an audio cassette so that I could play it on the portable cassette player I had taken to the hospital with me.

The first song, **Assault and Battery**, quickly became one of the many all-time favourites. It is still, to this day, played live by the band during their tours. It had, I thought, a most appropriate first verse. '*Lives of great men all remind us; we may make our lives sublime and departing leaves behind us, footprints in the sands of time.*'

Being in the situation that I was, facing an uncertain future, with so many variables racing through my mind, I felt this could have been written for me. Don't misunderstand; I am not for one second saying that I am a great man. Far from it, more the fact that it seemed that I was leaving my footprints, and nothing else in the sands of time, nothing else to show for my short time on earth.

Once this fourth cycle of chemotherapy was complete, I headed back to South Shields to await the arrival of my expected companions, sickness, lethargy, anorexia, isolation, and the inevitable psychological doubt.

In September 1975, I saw my team, Newcastle United, beat Aston Villa three goals to nil, which gave me a considerable lift. However, later that month, I made, perhaps, one of the most foolish decisions of my young life to that date. I was starting to feel quite well, the lumps, and bumps of lymphoma had vanished some weeks earlier. Therefore, in my humble, yet ignorant opinion, I decided that the four cycles of chemotherapy treatment had been sufficient, and there was no need to continue with this treatment, which was interfering with my life so drastically.

I decided enough was enough, even though Dr Sheppard had planned a further two cycles of treatment. I knew my body better than anyone, or did I? So, after only four cycles of chemotherapy, I took the monumental decision to stop treatment without consulting the Consultant or any of his team.

Having examined my body and found no lumps, I gave myself a clean bill of health and therefore, to my naïve and silly mind, the chemotherapy had been successful, and I had now finished the treatment that had caused untold upheaval in my young and as yet inexperienced life. It had robbed me of so many pleasures; altered my perceptions, both good and bad, made me bitter and mentally confused and placed me emotionally on a precipice.

So as the disease had controlled me for so long, I felt that it was long overdue that I took some control back. I foolishly failed to attend my next hospital appointment and even when a reminder came through the post a few days later, I ignored it. I felt that I had been living my life around cancer and that, in my view, wasn't right and in ignorance, I thought I would put the cancer experience behind me and with immediate effect! It was as easy as that, or so I thought.

Ten days later, early one evening, I was sitting at home watching television with my family — still trying to get my head around the notion that I had finished treatment and trying to be optimistic that my cancer would never return, when I heard a loud knock on the front door. To my surprise and amazement, standing there was my family doctor, larger than life, his twenty stone frame obscuring the natural light.

He immediately went into a rambling narration regarding the importance of starting the treatment again because if I didn't, I would be organizing my funeral. Not only was he, in my opinion, an incompetent doctor, he was also inept in his communication skills. What a bloody cheek coming to my front door and talking to me about funerals, but not just any funeral, my funeral.

In hindsight, he did, of course, have my best interest at heart and, I suppose, although I didn't see it at the time, I was blinkered by his previous inaccurate management of my illness. Not wanting to hear the truth, I asked him to go away with perhaps one or two expletives!

Naturally, my parents wanted to know what the raised voices were all about, and I remember feeling bad and so deceitful when Mam found out that essentially I had stopped the treatment of my own volition. As the tears rolled down her cheeks, my guilt surpassed stupidity, and tears of despondency filled my eyes.

I had let down not just my family, but also myself. I had failed to give myself the best opportunity of beating once and for all the lymphoma. Embarrassed as never before, I did the only thing I could, and that was to escape to the secluded confines of my bedroom.

Mentally, I tried to reflect on how the Lakota Sioux would cope with a situation like this, but, to no avail. Of all the chronicles of their plight and culture I had read, there was no description of managing a malignant disease.

I retired early to bed that night in September, and felt at perhaps my lowest ebb since discovering my diagnosis. I was upset that the doctor had been so brutally explicit regarding my future, and bewildered as to what course of action I should take now. During that endless night, I felt dismally lonely and confused like never before, but also very tearful and without a friend in the world to advise me on the correct course of action.

I was annoyed by the attempts of others to stifle my exposure to the truth and wanted control of my destiny or at the very least some say in it. But now that I had control, I found it more than difficult to make what potentially could be life or death decisions. I felt this was a no-win situation. I consciously did not discuss my deep and innermost emotions with my parents, simply because I knew the hurt it would cause, as they too would share my anguish.

I was not convinced I could honestly tolerate the onslaught of those drugs again, and the inevitable consequences they brought with them. If I explained this to my parents, they would be destroyed. With so much on my mind, I had very little sleep that night, but I think that I probably matured overnight, as I hesitantly decided the following morning that my future could only be guaranteed if I completed the despicable chemotherapy.

I reasoned that if the experts were recommending this barbaric treatment, then it must be necessary, they wouldn't put anyone through that just for the sake of it. I returned reluctantly to the Hospital on Thursday for my fifth course of those destructive drugs; acknowledging that once again, I would be living my life around cancer and I would no longer be in control.

To my surprise, the medical staff insisted that I have my scheduled treatment at the Diagnostic Centre at South Tyneside as an outpatient, rather than as an inpatient at Newcastle. I did wonder if the medical staff were now making an example of me because I had foolishly decided that four treatments were sufficient, but perhaps I was being relatively paranoid.

At times, it felt as if everything was conspiring against me and nothing appeared to go the way the medical team had expected. I couldn't understand how a treatment aimed at ridding your body of cancer would also damage everything in its path, my mind included! Sadly, the fear and anxiety about the expected side effects led me to feel nauseated even before I entered the premises, a feeling I knew all too well.

I can clearly remember feeling the sharp prick of the needle breach my skin and, almost immediately, the cold toxic substance being pushed along the syringe and into my fragile veins. Emotionally, I was wrecked, my mind was just buzzing with the fear and knowledge of what the consequence of this chemotherapy would bring, and I just could not face any more of this.

Once again, as had happened some months earlier, the Consultant stopped the treatment with little of the intended drugs delivered. It was not just his compassion and sincerity; it was also the empathy of the nursing sister who made me feel even more upset and tearful. My body trembled, my head was spinning, and I wept uncontrollably.

Only weeks earlier (August 1975), the Americans had launched the first of the Viking space rockets to Mars, where they would discover massive dry river beds — proof that the red planet had once hosted life. Such remarkable science and technology; yet, medical science could not find a treatment that would eliminate from my body an unwanted host, a cancer that was freely roaming around inside me.

Once again, transferred to Newcastle General Hospital and to the welcome embrace of ward 38 where a regimen of intravenous fluids and a similar cocktail of drugs that had worked quite well on my previous admission were being prepared. The chemotherapy treatment would not be given until the following day, as it was now early evening.

I was in hospital for a couple of days following the chemotherapy, and I deliberately did not leave the cubicle for fear of meeting anyone I had previously hoped I would see. My unbalanced mental state was not ready for peer support, and their reciprocal empathy, yet ironically, I missed that support.

Dr Sheppard came in to see me on Monday morning, and told me I would be going home, and that because of my inability to tolerate the cytotoxic chemotherapy, this fifth course would be my last, but — then came a massive shock!

Sitting on the side of my bed, Dr Sheppard told me that there was still evidence of lymphoma, and it was very unlikely that the amount of chemotherapy that I had received would be sufficient to control this highly aggressive cancer.

He looked straight into my eyes, and said with conviction, '*There is less chance of getting rid of this cancer than previously thought, but as you have relapsed, we must try.*'

Therefore, he had decided on an alternative treatment. One that was gentler but would complement what had already been given. Despite this unwelcome prognosis, I admired, at last, his honesty and openness and asked for some detail on what this alternative treatment was.

The new regimen would include some oral chemotherapy tablets called Cyclophosphamide, taken for fourteen days. In addition, I would be required to take more steroids. But most importantly, another component would be a drug called Bleomycin, which was administered as an injection into the muscle of my bottom.

It was planned to have the injections twice each week for two weeks — this would be repeated every four weeks. What did I have to lose, it didn't sound too harsh and what's more, the Consultant had said that if I felt up to it, then I could return to work and have the on-site doctor administer the injections. To my frustration, the doctor at Readhead's Shipyard decided he wanted nothing to do with this chemotherapy, and it was therefore left to my family doctor to give the injections — yes him!

In fairness, he did not appear to hold any grudges following our verbal confrontation a few weeks earlier, and the treatment went uneventfully. The treatment wasn't too bad in comparison to what I had previously been given, and it did allow me to get back to work, which was important to me as it would give me some normality and social interaction.

Hopes of joining the Royal Navy were now forlorn, and yet, despite being happy at work, I found it very taxing and at the end of my working day, I simply had no energy for anything else other than sleep. The intramuscular injections were bloody painful and meant you couldn't sit for about an hour afterward. Fortunately, this treatment only lasted for two weeks, after which I would then have a four-week break before commencing the next cycle.

Thankfully, after two cycles of this most unusual of treatments, and after a physical examination, no lymph nodes could be detected, and my blood count was normal. Dr Sheppard felt that I was in remission.

'*Was I cured*?' I tentatively asked.

His reply resonated throughout my head, '*Too early to say that, I'm afraid.*'

On my way home, his words swam in different directions around my mind. So, from my diagnosis in May, I was now coming to the end of a journey that began with the mishandling of my symptoms. I underwent many unpleasant investigations, experienced the devastating psychological effects of the unknown, and felt betrayed and undermined by the attempts to keep my diagnosis from me.

The trials and tribulations of dealing with chemotherapy led to many mixed emotions; the optimism of recovery and then the depressive decline of realizing that your very existence was always under threat. All of this culminated in my foolish decision to end my treatment in September. At last, now the treatment was finished, perhaps I could at this moment put this whole chapter of my life behind me.

It was such a relief, yet I felt somewhat isolated and vulnerable, gone was the safety net of the hospital. Although I would be back and forward for check-ups, it would not be the intensive contact I'd been used to. I would also miss the camaraderie and support of Tom and the other patients whom I had met at Newcastle General Hospital, and the welcome embrace of ward 38.

I felt that it was most important to get back to work, purely and simply to normalize my life, but to prove that the cancer was not going to dictate what I could and couldn't do in my life. On my return to Readhead's shipyard, I was asked to schedule an appointment with one of the training officers.

In his office, I was told that the management had decided that because of my '*serious condition*' (his inability to say the word cancer), then it wasn't practical for me to return to welding, and I was allocated to the plating shed. This job was cleaner and also presented less toxic fumes.

My time in the shipyards was enjoyable. The industry was full of weird and wonderful characters. People such as Mickey F****** Broon, so named because between every other word he used the 'F' word. He called me F****** shite hawk, his reason? '*He likes Hawkwind, and he's full of F****** shite.*'

I have no idea where he got his rationale from, but he was a harmless guy. Jimmy the carthorse, my previous manager (the one who caught me asleep in the cofferdams) came up to me to ask how I was.

I think he felt bad about the verbal rollicking he had given me that day and said, '*You should have said you were poorly.*'

The truth was, of course, I did not realize how poorly I was, and I felt quite sorry for Jimmy that day. Word had quickly spread throughout this small shipyard of my diagnosis, and many of the older men in the shipyard tried to come and speak with me that afternoon. That was important to me, even those men who hardly knew me suddenly adopted me as a friend.

The management at Readhead's shipyard were very supportive of my situation. If I wanted or needed time off work, then I only had to say the word. It was a good time, a time when life appeared to be getting back to normal, or so I thought. As always, in the back of my mind was the inevitable fear of cancer and the worry about how long I would be well.

Soon, very soon, I would have that answer.

In the interim, for the sake of my mental health, I had to put those dreaded thoughts to the back of my mind and get on with life. Fishing would also prove to be an escape mechanism. Neil, also from the shipyards, was a good friend, and we'd spend many a night sitting on the edge of the rocks at Marsden fishing.

More importantly, when I'd go to his house, his wife, Jean, would be there. Jean was a staff nurse and I had developed a considerable admiration for the work that they did, and I felt this was something I would like to do. At that time, I had no qualifications, nor was I ready to leave a relatively well-paid job in the shipyard for a career in nursing. But talk of nursing excited and interested me, and I imagined how much better it would be to have a fulfilling and rewarding career, rather than the mundane life in a shipyard.

Fishing expeditions with Neil would become regular occurrences; I clearly remember one night sitting on the rock edges peering into the black wilderness way out to sea, and seeing a shooting star diving towards the earth. I'm sure there is no need to explain what I wished for that night.

Between treatments, my friend Robbo, and I would spend many nights at the City Hall in Newcastle seeing a whole host of different bands; it helped marginalize the deviation from normality. It gave me a sense of acceptance, doing the things that normal adolescents do. By Christmas 1975, I felt better than I had for some time, and I was getting out and about with some of my friends.

I knew their eagle eyes were constantly focused on me, and ready to protect me should the need arise; although fortunately, it never was. More and more people would come up to me and ask how I was, even those that I didn't know too well. I appreciated this, recognition on my behalf that people were truly, well-intentioned, and that the world wasn't such a bad place after all.

It was around this juncture in time that I realized what I'd missed over the past year, and I now enjoyed the social scene and felt quite optimistic. Unfortunately, my optimism was short-lived, as mid-way through April 1976 I began to feel unwell. It was less than six-months since I had finished treatment. But, the tell-tale signs began to appear. The lumps under my arms indicated only one thing, the cancer was back again!

I had no other option but to contact the hospital, and bring forward my appointment. The sweats had once again started to pay me nightly visits, and I was experiencing specific chest pains. The drugs, Bleomycin and Cyclophosphamide, had failed to halt the determined advancement of this obstinate cancer. What would their approach be now? Would they have another approach?

Perhaps as a believer in fate, then I had to accept that my existence was not intended to be a long one and that eventually, this cancer would ultimately terminate my life. At the hospital, the obligatory blood test and physical examination confirmed that the lymphoma was once again becoming active and that further treatment would be required.

At least, I thought to myself — they were not giving up, even though I had an inherent fear of the treatment they proposed. I was told that there is a swollen gland in the left axilla and at least a couple in the groin. This represented a second relapse, and as if they hadn't learned anything about communication the first time around, my Mam and Dad were taken to one side, and told that it will now prove more difficult to control what is an aggressive lymphoma. In addition, it meant that the original chances of a fifty percent chance of survival would be significantly reduced.

During our discussions many years later, Mam confided that it would not be uncommon for her to cry uncontrollably, and unexpectedly, such was her and my father's worry about my condition. An inherent fear of losing their only son. Their helplessness at not being able to assist me to rid my body of the demon inside and its controlling effects was difficult for them to accept.

It was now that I expressed abhorrence at being confronted by more chemotherapy, and I did not want this. To this end, I told the registrar, who had informed me that the disease was once again progressing. I told him, that I could not guarantee that I would be strong enough to complete further treatment.

However, when he said that I would be going to Newcastle for further treatment — it meant only one thing, I was going to get radiotherapy. Despite the fact, that he never actually came out and said that. It was my way of coping, my twisted mind making the wrong interpretation of what he had said.

I had seen other patients tolerate this radiotherapy treatment when I was at Newcastle, and it appeared to be absent of side effects, so I agreed to attend ward 38 again the following day.

Amazingly, at times we hear what we want to hear and exclude everything else. What's more surprising is the fact that we believe it too. This was one of those very examples.

On the ward, I found that things were no different than I remembered. The same nurses were there but, unfortunately, there were no familiar faces among the other patients. The junior doctor on duty asked me the repetitive questions that I knew so well, and then he proceeded to tell me that the chemotherapy would start later in the afternoon.

'*Hang on there!*' I said. '*I'm not here for chemotherapy, I'm having radiotherapy.*'

The young doctor looked bewildered, checked the medical notes and being somewhat confused trotted off to the office to clarify exactly what treatment would be given.

Almost immediately, along came Syd, one of the staff nurses that, by now, I knew very well. Syd tried to explain that chemotherapy had been planned for me and because my cancer was quite widespread throughout the body, then radiotherapy wasn't an option. At that point I became upset, I felt betrayed and let down. If that was all that was on offer then thanks but no, thanks. I was adamant I was not having more unforgiving chemotherapy.

I simply did not feel I could cope with all the physical, and mental torture that accompanied that treatment, particularly as it offered no guarantee of a cure. I can recall clearly that Syd was taken aback by my response, but he then carried on telling me that this was my only option. But my mind was made up; I would not, could not accept more of this gruelling chemotherapy.

Syd sat at the bedside and spoke slowly and concisely, purposely and carefully choosing his words, delivering each sentence with genuine empathy, '*If you don't have the treatment you may not survive this cancer.*'

His blunt, but honest, and accurate words echoed around my head. In the first instance, I felt anger towards Syd, thinking that it was easy for him to sit there and say that. It was not him stuck with this bloody cancer racing around his body, and facing further chemical torment. Almost immediately I felt guilty for having those thoughts, he was only trying to help, and it certainly could not have been easy to sit beside me, not knowing how I would respond.

At this point, I made perhaps the most important decision of my life. '*I am not having further chemotherapy and, if I have to die, then that's it.*' My decision was final, yet strangely, I did not find this decision difficult to make; on the contrary, I felt a gigantic burden lifted from my shoulders. Surprisingly, even to me, I remained very calm, but I do remember feeling sorrowful for my family.

It is difficult trying to convey this concept to anyone because people may say that you would cling to every opportunity and grasp any chance you have in life and yes, of course, some people would do that. However, the emotional turmoil, debilitating nausea, the gut-wrenching vomiting, and the psychological confusion were beyond comprehension, the depressive isolation intolerable.

Anticipating how you're going to feel before it's even started was something I felt was not an option I was prepared to accept. Syd, however, not to be beaten, asked if we could discuss things in a more private setting, and although I was adamant that I was not having chemotherapy, I agreed to his request.

He did not try and directly persuade me to have more chemotherapy, instead he spoke of how he could not even begin to imagine what the treatment was like, and I respected his honest approach. He also spoke of my family, and the effect my decision would have on them. Eventually, after almost an hour, Syd, in some psychological process, convinced me that chemotherapy was the route to take, and so I very reluctantly agreed to further treatment.

I'm unsure if Syd realized exactly the monumental change of heart he had instigated that day, but one thing is for certain, he inspired me to continue, and I do not believe many others could have done that. Syd would leave nursing, and take up a role in social work, and I would never see him again.

Curiously, I often wonder what might have been if he had not been on duty that day, I do not believe that many other nurses or indeed doctors back then would have talked so openly and honestly about death as Syd did with me. If you happen to read this Syd, I owe you so much, and thank you.

I believe that in many regards, some nurses and indeed some doctors working in the demanding field of cancer care become therapeutic friends to patients. It is difficult to see sometimes where this relationship starts, and where it ends, or does it ever end? What is certain is the fact that without these therapeutic friends, cancer patients would be lost.

Subsequently, for me, it was chemotherapy time again. The dosages would be reduced from what had previously been given due to my inability to cope with the wrath of this infernal but necessary therapy. Some specific drugs would be changed from what I'd previously received, as it was pointless giving the same drugs again when the disease had become so active so quickly.

The junior doctor told me that before more treatment was given, I would require a blood transfusion. However, due to all the treatment, and all the subsequent needles, it was becoming increasingly more difficult to locate good veins. The veins in my upper limbs were proving unresponsive, so after a third attempt to gain venous access, the needle for the blood transfusion was inserted into my foot.

This, of course, restricted my mobility, and I was stuck lying on top of the bed. After the blood transfusion, the same needle was flushed with saline and used for my chemotherapy, although the toxic poison was infused through a different line. Unfortunately for me, despite a different cocktail of drugs, the treatment was pretty similar to what I had received the previous year and the side effects were just as I'd remember them, horrific!

Time seemed to go nowhere; yet it seemed to last forever. One day merged into the next with little respite from nausea, and a general lethargy. Chemotherapy had started again on 28 May 1976, almost one year exactly since my diagnosis. Treatment was planned as regularly as possible, depending upon the recovery of my healthy cells.

The expectation was, that the chosen chemotherapy treatment would be administered at twenty-one day intervals, although from time to time, twenty-one days between treatments was simply not enough time for my healthy cells to recover, and it would be delayed a further week. This, of course, was depressing as it meant I could not see an end to my unwanted nightmare.

However, these deferrals were essential. The chemotherapy could have easily, although indirectly, taken my life from me. Had my white cell count not increased sufficiently between treatments, my immune system could not function adequately, and I would be at risk of life-threatening opportunistic infection.

Of course, I had some difficulty understanding this concept, and I was very frustrated as any delays simply prolonged my agony. All I wanted to do was get on with it so that, hopefully, I could put whatever treatment was planned behind me. Yet, the unappeasable chemotherapy left no part of me untouched.

One morning I awoke to discover a weird rash covering the left side of my body, with pain like electrical impulses shocking my feeble frame. The doctor quickly diagnosed Shingles. The ruthless consequences of cancer treatment increased my mental anguish at yet another setback. I would rather not be receiving chemotherapy, but what choice did I have?

My sanity was saved partially by reading about the social injustices, and the attempted destruction of the Lakota Nation. It made me realize that there is always someone worse than I was. I loved reading about the culture of the Sioux Empire, and I still had hopes of visiting Wounded Knee someday.

My sleep pattern was not great at the best of the times, but the shingle's infection was causing additional problems, and my mind was now in overdrive thinking that this nightmare was never going to end.

What the hell was happening to my body? And when, if ever, would I regain control? I was given some medication, and told to restrict myself to the house, which further impacted my quality of life. My biggest problem was the suppression of my normal thoughts, the inability to rationalize or comprehend why this was happening.

The weeks came and went, each day merged into the next, and time was of little relevance any longer. The hospital setting became my second home, and the staff part of my extended family. Despite that supportive network and, of course, not forgetting my biological family, chemotherapy treatment was no easier to accept psychologically than it was to receive physically.

There was an uneasy nervousness, a predictable fear leading up to every treatment, knowing fine well that following on from the predatory chemotherapy my body no longer had any respect for what it was that I wanted it to do. It would be controlled by the effects of the lifesaving drugs. It was as if my body were bereft of vitality, the vigour drained from within by an unrelenting attack.

The known consequences made it far less easy to accept, and waiting, and anticipating the side effects made life intolerable for a teenager in the seventies. Would there ever be an end to this purgatory?

I felt as though I was becoming a submissive entity with nothing more than an unheard voice. I had no concerns about the physical care I was receiving. My views, feelings, or wishes were never considered, and although my best interests were always at the forefront, what about my worries? What about my needs, the loss of my identity, and my worries, who would address these important issues?

A cloud of blackness would obscure my mind when I least expected, and I found it a difficult demon to control. There were no support groups, no specialist nurses. Almost no one was willing to speak with me about cancer — fearing addressing the psychological unrest it was causing me; the risk it was posing to my existence. It felt like a one-man battle, and I did not believe that I was winning this most decisive war.

Eventually, some five months down the line and the infernal cocktail of treatment was thankfully once again complete. However, now that the treatment was again terminated, I started to plan my return to full-time employment and, more importantly, attend the next Hawkwind concert. The latter took place in September 1976 at Newcastle City Hall, and it would prove a spectacular event, with an equally amazing light show to match the fantastic space rock that only Hawkwind could provide.

Additionally, the band's tour was still in full swing around the country and after this show, I was determined to ensure I saw them again. Therefore, I arranged the necessary payment for the scheduled performance of Hawkwind at the famous Hammersmith Odeon the following month. I planned to make my way to the big city and demonstrate my support for the band.

Less than a week later, that all-important ticket arrived, making me wonder if life was finally returning to normal. Once again, it would not be too long before I got the answer, but sadly not the answer I expected. I was back at work, and the Readhead's shipyard in South Shields was preparing to close down and transfer its workforce to other yards along the River Tyne.

I was no exception, and I was allocated a place at Swan Hunters at Wallsend. I remember my first day as if it were yesterday. As I walked into the new department, my hair still absent, a concrete reminder that my health was far from certain. One man's offensive comment to another person was just a little too loud, and I overheard his sarcastic criticism of my strange hairstyle.

I was hurt, and offended that another man could make light of my current predicament. Without a pause in my stride, I continued along, pretending that I had not heard his remarks. As I walked, I thought of the proud Lakota Sioux warriors and their long threads of hair, which were such an important part of their identity. Mine had been too, but it had been taken from me by a hidden scourge.

Only a week later, in total despair, I knew I had to cancel my trip to London as once again, I was aware of those tell-tale signs of recurrence of cancer, and the associated feelings that went hand in hand with them. I knew that it would not be possible to make the long journey to London feeling the way I did, tired, and emotionally on edge. Those drenching night sweats, informing me that my unwanted accomplice was yet again returning for a further, uninvited visit.

I had missed Newcastle United defeating Stoke City by a single goal in our last game — and now sitting in my bedroom, staring at my unused ticket for the Hammersmith Odeon, it left me tearful, and frustrated, and once again wondering what the immediate future had in store for me. My next appointment was a few weeks away, and in all honesty, I should have contacted the hospital to bring it forward as I knew exactly what was occurring deep within my body.

Instead, I foolishly waited. Completely bewildered, and mentally unstable, near to a complete psychological breakdown.

I went to bed, and lay across the duvet, and closed my eyes, hoping to sleep. But the dominant demons were there instantly. They hounded my thoughts, controlled my mind, and reminded me of my life-threatening disease that continued to circulate around my body. The entity I could not control insisted on invading my psychological wellbeing, tipping it into imbalance.

Feeling depressed, and isolated, I trudged along to my scheduled appointment early in November 1976 more terrified than ever as to what management strategy would now be initiated. Frustratingly, it was my first clinic appointment since completing the last chemotherapy, and although deep down I knew what was happening, I paradoxically prayed that I would get a clean bill of health.

It's crazy how as individuals we try to convince ourselves that things are going well, and I desperately wanted to be well. Sadly, and as expected, my worst fears were realized, and they confirmed that I had relapsed a third time, and explained that there had been only a partial response to the chemotherapy. This came as no surprise at all, but it was the worst news I could wish to hear.

A lymph node was quite evident in my right axilla accompanied by others in my chest, and I was told, as I expected, that more treatment would be required. I was, perhaps for the first time in my life, speechless, gutted, bewildered, and confused as to where we go from here as I had pinned so much hope on the last chemotherapy that I had reluctantly accepted. My immediate response was one of anger.

I now felt more vulnerable than ever before, I also felt that perhaps, as a believer in destiny, my end was in sight. So here I was again, I had clawed and dragged my way to the top, only to be cruelly pushed back to the bottom of this rollercoaster of emotional and physical disturbance. Dark thoughts circling in my subconscious left me embarrassed by an inclination to end my life.

Mentally weakened by this expected news, I thought of a simple way to end my torture and indeed, my life. But how and who would find me? I cried with self-pity, I sobbed with anger and frustration. I knew that I was not strong enough to end it all, to leave a legacy for my parents and my sister that would surely haunt them forever.

In my despair, my thoughts turned to the Lakota Sioux struggles and exploitation over the decades, and their pride and steely determination was an attribute that had and would inspire me. The Lakota men would often paint their faces for personal protection before they went into battle with an enemy.

But the ceremonial culture of face painting was more than that, the chosen colours were of individual choice, intended to harmonize that person's dreams and visions. My battle was once again about to begin, I needed to put to one side the demons that lurked in the canyons of my mind and visualize my future and recognize the dreams I needed to attain.

Despite feeling very much alone, I was mentally strengthened by the thought that I was accompanied on my journey by the Lakota Sioux; dismissing the weak and destructive thoughts of suicide for the moment.

My fragile emotions, and worries would belong to me, and me alone, as I felt that my parents, and sister did not deserve to have to share this burden. A burden I could not manage myself. I knew how difficult my family were finding the whole ordeal, and subsequently, I kept this personal turmoil inside as a protective factor in favour of them.

Of course, in hindsight that was a mistake, as I struggled constantly to deal with the fears, and strange dilemmas that would invade my mind daily. Questions my subconscious would ask of me, questions I would refuse to answer. I had no answers to the myriad of self-posed questions, and, in reality; it would have helped if I'd shared some of that responsibility.

After all, this wasn't just my cancer, it impinged the entire family, and they deserved the opportunity to help me. Yet in absolute naivety, I denied them that chance and also myself the support that it would have brought. I suppose, in essence, the fact remains that there is no preparation for the fight against cancer, whether it is you the individual or a member of your family.

No one person can say what you should or shouldn't do; it remains the ultimate discovery of your inner self. A discovery that is made during the lonely and unpredictable road of the cancer journey, and I was no exception.

This was the third relapse and had dire consequences. Once again, I began to acknowledge and yet at the same time, question my mortality. Would I ever be in a position to father a child and see them grow up, had I seen Hawkwind perform for the last time, would I ever get to Wounded Knee?

My mind was filled with the never-ending worry as to exactly what fate had in store for me, and concerns whether this disease would end my life. Questions rolled around my mind almost constantly and, yet, no one could offer any answers. My fate was woven into the intricate tapestry of life.

Perhaps my biggest problem was the fact that as a young and immature man, I had always chosen not to discuss much of my illness or even discuss the savage games played out in my mind to anyone.

From the beginning, I had made the conscious decision to keep my thoughts, my fears, and my questions to myself; aware that my parents who had colluded with the doctor to withhold information about my illness, were struggling to understand, and confront the fact that their son had cancer — a life-limiting disease.

Chapter 6
Merry Christmas

I first met Dr Bozzino, a Consultant Oncologist, and Dr Atkinson, a Specialist Registrar, when they took over my care from Dr Sheppard. He had accepted a new Consultancy in Australia, although he would be around for a little while. Subsequently, Dr Bozzino proposed that radiotherapy should be used as the next treatment option.

The medical team knew very well that I was opposed to more chemotherapy, and although many may see that as my weakness, I simply could not have tolerated any more of the infernal solution that had desecrated my entire body. Especially as there was no guarantee that further chemotherapy would work.

Radiotherapy would, of course, also bring with it, unknown challenges but, presently, I was just relieved that there was an alternative treatment available to me, and one which, I thought, would not give me the dreadful side effects I had from the chemotherapy. At least that was my perception.

I was asked to make my way once again to Newcastle General Hospital to get prepared for radiotherapy, and I was told that this treatment would be delivered as an outpatient, and that an ambulance would take me back and forth to Newcastle each day — Monday to Friday, for five weeks.

The consultant explained that radiotherapy is a treatment that is given to localized disease. That is to say, it is aimed at getting rid of cancer in one specific area, whereas chemotherapy is a systemic option, it would get into every nook and cranny of the human anatomy. That was the main reason why radiotherapy had not been considered for my condition before now; they needed a treatment that would attack the widespread nature of my cancer.

Why on earth this was never explained to me months ago is anyone's guess; it would have made perfect sense and perhaps would have softened my anger at not being considered for radiotherapy before now. From a cynical viewpoint, I wondered if they thought that as a young adolescent, I was incapable of comprehending this simple explanation, but that quickly became history as I focused on starting radiotherapy.

Radiotherapy is administered much like a simple X-ray, but with one crucial difference — a significantly higher dose of radiation. However, it isn't as simple as aiming a beam at the affected area; strict precautions are necessary, as this radiation can cause long-term damage to healthy tissues.

To protect my lungs from the harmful effects of ionizing radiation, special metal blocks were crafted. This form of radiotherapy, known as mantle irradiation, was designed to minimize collateral damage. The first session was surprisingly easy, lasting only a few minutes.

Before treatment began, my skin was marked — patterns that reminded me of a Lakota warrior. The thought amused me, though I felt nothing like a warrior. Still, it was an unexpected connection to my Lakota friends — friends I had never met, the Lakota Sioux who lived thousands of miles away. Yet, in my heart, they were close, their unseen presence a silent support in my psychological battle.

These markings allowed radiographers to position me in exactly the correct position on the treatment couch for each of the daily treatments. Of course, like most of the treatments for cancer, the side effects were often more potent than the actual disease and radiotherapy was no exception. Just like chemotherapy, it would damage healthy cells while it destroyed lymphoma cells too.

Unknown to me and my naive intellect, the treatment, would prove not to be without side effects. It had been me, who had persistently argued and insisted on having radiotherapy, having seen all of those other chaps receive this form of treatment at Newcastle. As I saw it, it seemed free of side effects.

The first three weeks of radiotherapy went without any problem. However, eventually, the treatment began to take its savage toll on my young and innocent body. At first, these side effects crept up on me very gradually. Firstly, the tiredness left me so fatigued that I would feel the need to sleep for at least a couple of hours on my return from hospital.

Secondly, my throat became hoarse and I had difficulty swallowing. Soon afterwards, the sickness started and proved just as difficult to control as the chemotherapy-induced sickness. The plan was for twenty-three treatments consisting of a total of 3436 rads (a measure of radiation), to the chest and neck, with a final booster of 500 rads to my entire upper body — that, is a fair whack of radiation.

At the Newcastle hospital where the radiotherapy was delivered, the small waiting area was crammed wall to wall with patient's waiting to receive their treatment. A constant production line is precisely what you do not want when you are feeling low in mood, tired, and just wanting to be anywhere other than a hospital.

At times, I felt trapped in a permanent nightmare with no ending, thinking to myself, at least if I died that would be a release, but instead I'm alive, and stuck with this unbearable burden of cancer. Christmas 1976 was, undoubtedly, the worst Christmas of my entire life.

My get-up and go, got up of its own volition, and left me bereft of vigour, drained of enthusiasm, and in the depths of despair. Persecuted by an illness I could not see and, more importantly, that I had no control over. Ironically, I was now learning to respect this potential killer disease that was proving rather difficult to eradicate. Its persistence to return, and invade my body, its refusal to respond to conventional treatment, and the difficulty modern medicine had in ridding my body of this disease was a considerable concern.

To make matters worse, I found that my appetite was perhaps the worst thing affected, perhaps due to the constant feeling of nausea. Everything I tried to eat tasted like soggy cardboard, and my Mam was concerned and tried all kinds of tempting dishes with little success. She even went out and bought a build-up drink to try to tempt my taste buds.

Now here is a strange concept, if I am not eating then the last thing I would want is some bland, tasteless unappetizing drink, even though it was supposed to deliver the nutritional support I was lacking. Sadly, the drink was indeed bland and tasteless and something that succeeded in exacerbating my nausea. As much as I appreciated Mam's attempt to build me up, that approach was simply not for me.

To make matters worse, as the radiotherapy exerted its effect on the disease in my chest, the pains I experienced were excruciating. They would manifest when I least expected them and caused me to freeze with discomfort and fear — fear that this was the progression of the lymphoma. I had been prescribed strong painkillers, but even these had unwanted side effects.

I became constipated, and they caused my head to spin as if I had consumed an entire bottle of my favourite Bourbon, '*Jim Beam.*' The pain would be worse at night when I was alone, compounded by the silence — the darkness, the isolation and, of course, my trepidation of what lay ahead.

I felt lost and persecuted by an uninvited entity inside my body that refused to leave me. Radiotherapy continued until 28th January 1977, through what was a freezing winter with plenty of snow on the ground.

Trying to get motivated, I remember going for short walks in the snow at night, often around midnight when no one was around — alone with my negative thoughts, and not knowing in which direction to turn. I think, in all honesty, it was at this stage that I felt sorrier for myself than at any other time. I was aware that all of my friends would be out enjoying themselves, and although they regularly called in during the day to see me — nighttime was different. It was a constant reminder that I was not living a normal life.

I was isolated from society, unable to participate in the activities of any normal adolescent, battling an unseen disease that refused to release me from its deathly stranglehold. Not only that, but I was still not eating, and I began to lose weight, which concerned not only my parents but also the medical staff. At one point, Dr Bozzino confessed that he was considering stopping the radiotherapy due to his concerns over my weight loss, although in his wisdom he eventually decided against that course of action.

I previously mentioned that during my darkest moments, I had thoughts of ending my life, and you might wonder how often I had felt that way. I can say that it was on more than one occasion, and that is a fact that I am not ashamed to admit. The thought of ending my life did not just cause me personal grief and consternation, it made me feel guilty, as I knew the devastation it would cause my family.

Without any warning whatsoever, dark thoughts would wander, unopposed and uninvited, through the canyons of my mind — a cloak of uncertainty and suggestions that my young head was unable to understand or comprehend. Not for the first time, I turned to the inspirational Lakota Sioux and, in particular, a Holy man called '*Black Elk.*'

His editorial about his persecution and his resolve and his unexplained visions, which gave him direction in life, spurred me on and out of the spiralling depressive mind-set. Deep inside my head, his words resonated and something inside me said, *you will survive.* Regardless, I am uncertain whether I would have had the courage to carry out that fateful deed.

Unlike today, when I was treated with radiotherapy you were not allowed to wash the area being treated and subsequently, I developed a large '*tide*' mark around the back of my neck where my collars would rub. Additionally, I had not had a bath for the entire duration of the treatment and my hair had not been washed for the same period.

The suggestion was that both your hair and skin could be cleaned with talcum powder. Of course, I am confident that everyone can appreciate that this does not work the same as good old soap and water. I felt filthy and lord only knows what pungent aroma I would be giving off? Joking aside, no one ever gave me the slightest indication that there was a problem with my hygiene. It was also the time of the good old '*Brut*' aftershave adverts on television, and Christmas had brought me my fair share of the smelly cologne.

Therefore, every morning religiously during the radiotherapy days, I would splash it all over! After completing my radiotherapy, I had to wait a further fourteen days before I could bathe, as the radiation was still effective on my skin for that duration. Eventually, though, the day arrived, and my Mam had filled the most inviting bath I had ever wished for.

Tentatively I dipped my toes in as if I were an alien visiting a strange land and having my first experience of water. I lay there smiling to myself and soaked my skin to a prune until the water became only tepid. Despite my long, and relaxing soak, the tidemark remained for some weeks thereafter, and this was a great source of ridicule by my Mother. She made it her business to tell everyone about the now-famous tidemark around my neck.

Despite the seriousness and gravity of the situation, it was good to laugh. I hadn't done a lot of laughing up to this point. I felt alive, content, and almost normal but not quite.

As the weeks progressed, I began to get stronger and stronger and began to get the urge to return to work. I also began to dream about visiting America and an Indian reservation. I had been keeping in regular contact with Aunty Mary, and the offer to visit was permanently on the table. My hospital visits continued at monthly intervals to monitor my blood counts and undergo the usual physical examinations which were a prerequisite to every visit.

As the time progressed during these, my formative years, I matured rather quickly and appreciated that life was not only important but also precious. I soon deduced that for the majority of people, life was taken for granted and yet more than anyone I now knew how special life was. Seeing individual after individual abuse themselves, I had no doubt, that had illness not intervened, and then I too would have been just another person who did not respect the sanctity of life.

I was slowly but surely earning more and more respect for this cancer, but equally accepting that it was teaching me a very valuable lesson about life; enjoy it while you can, as we won't be here forever. Things went well for some weeks but, soon, things took an almost expected downward plunge. Some seven weeks after completing my radiotherapy, I discovered a lump under my left arm and knew exactly what this meant, lymphoma! More importantly, it also meant the prospect of more treatment.

This represented a fourth relapse, and immediately my mood sunk to a new low. I imagined that perhaps my life was not destined to be a long one. I desperately did not want to allow these depressive feelings to take over my mind, and once again I searched for motivation. It is critical to highlight that my family were a vitally significant component in my life, especially during my illness.

But the factual events I read about the Lakota people and to a lesser extent, the music of Hawkwind gave me the element of escapism and distraction that I was seeking; a connection with spirituality and with my soul, which is difficult to explain to someone who has not faced their own mortality. My mood followed peaks and troughs of uncontrollable dimensions, and emotional instability.

Twelve months earlier, I would have shuddered at the thought of more chemotherapy and the potential dangers that it brought with it. But now, I was desperately hoping more treatment would be offered as I was determined to cling to life as I knew that I had so much to live for. I also had my family to consider.

They were right behind me and supported me to the very best of their ability. They felt my pain and shared my anguish as if it were their own. I knew I had their undivided support, but, equally, I knew that refusing further treatment would be the ultimate self-destruction that might also destroy them. I never saw Dr Sheppard again, but my parents did!

Now, it's easy to be critical of my parents, and their collusion with the medical establishment, but I know for certain how they too struggled mentally with my cancer diagnosis. They were, or tried, to be very protective, whilst at the same time, I was trying to adjust to life outside of cancer.

I was desperate to get out and about, not just to see live music, but to socialize with my dependable and supportive friends. My life was still of course governed by cancer and the effects of the treatment, and I understood my frailty was still recovering. However, I accepted and knew that each one of my friends would watch over me whenever we were together. I also appreciated the confidence and comfort that their friendship and support brought me.

But, it was a peculiar emotion I experienced; whilst their support sometimes felt like protectionism, they gave this with the best of intentions. I felt that I had lost my adolescence. I felt that because of their protection, I was not normal.

Unknown to me and as if they had not learned anything from the first time, my parents met with Dr. Sheppard one afternoon, only a week before he was due to leave — they were told that it was not now possible to control this aggressive lymphoma. He further explained that from a medical prognosis, it was only a matter of time until I died as a consequence of this stubborn, and unresponsive cancer.

The plan, therefore, from that moment was palliative treatment, which was intended to control my symptoms, but significantly would not cure the lymphoma! The decision was made without my consent, nothing new there then! However, here is the ethical dilemma, if I had been told that I was not expected to survive, would I have accepted the offer of further chemotherapy? I suspect not. But, that is the paradox.

One important factor in the history of my illness is the use of complementary therapy. My Mam had been reading about this wonder root called Ginseng and the significant improvement it could make to the human body. The book she had read, claimed that the root could improve life and rid the body of many conditions and ailments, although I do not believe it claimed to treat cancer.

Nevertheless, she duly went out and bought a supply of this herb, and each day I would regimentally take one capsule. Until her dying day, Mam insisted this herbal root played a significant role in my recovery. Previously, when I returned to work following the radiotherapy, I struggled to complete a full five days, and, at times, I would only manage two or three days.

The management, on the whole, were very supportive; their suggestion to me was, come in when you feel well enough. I was never certain whether Mam or Dad had spoken to anyone at work to inform them of how ill I was. However, I truly appreciated the fact that work was flexible with my hours. It was a valuable element, both from a financial perspective, but also to normalize my life again, and I endeavoured to get into work at every opportunity.

Despite my relentless tiredness, my thoughts were focused on the next Hawkwind tour, where would that be, and would I manage to get there? At my next clinic appointment, Dr Bozzino spoke to me directly and listened to me, allowing me the time to ask specific questions.

I am not saying that Dr Sheppard had not spoken to me previously, he had done and he was an excellent doctor. I just felt that he mostly collaborated with my parents about my disease and my management. After all, this was my cancer and I felt he had previously attempted, although well-intentioned, to take it away from me and remove my role in the decision-making process.

Dr Bozzino was an articulate and pleasant gentleman, who made me feel very relaxed. His time was my time and importantly, he made time to ensure that I was able to ask all the questions that I needed. His eternal optimism was heart-warming, even though he knew something that I did not. Dr Atkinson would also have a special place in my heart, for reasons that will soon become apparent.

He was a tall Englishman with an excellent disposition, someone who enjoyed a good laugh, someone I could relate to, empathetic and professional, and I developed the utmost respect for both men. At that consultation, I was told that I'd had a fair response to the radiotherapy, but there was a node under my arm and some lymph nodes deep in the abdomen which had not been treated by the radiotherapy and, therefore, needed to be targeted by other treatment.

Unbeknown to me, what this amounted to was palliative chemotherapy to improve my quality of life, but would not cure my cancer. This was something that had already been discussed with my parents, but not me! Whether Dr Bozzino, and Dr Atkinson were aware of that collusion between Dr Sheppard, and my parents I was never certain, I prefer to believe that they did not, but honestly, suspect they did.

I was told that I was to have weekly injections, which would be almost free from side effects. This was certainly something that impressed me immediately. But was this possible, no side effects from chemotherapy? I doubted that very much. I later learned that the reason there were fewer side effects was that this type of treatment is weaker, as it is intended to resolve some of my symptoms and push the disease into the background, not to cure it.

Furthermore, I was asked to go for a coffee until the drug could be ordered from the pharmacy, and I was happy to oblige. I had received a lot of information from these two doctors, and, most importantly, I was being involved in the decision-making process. I saw no reason to question this next course of action.

I wandered around to the WRVS coffee bar.

An hour or so later, one of the nurses came looking for me to say that Dr Bozzino was now ready for me. I was subsequently whisked straight back into the consulting room that I know so very well. Dr Bozzino had a butterfly needle in the back of my hand and secured it into position before I knew it.

The drug, called Vinblastine was administered in no time at all and the needle was swiftly removed, and I was on my way home before I knew it. Over the next

85

three months, I attended the outpatient department to see either Dr Atkinson or Dr Bozzino and to receive my Vinblastine injection. The dose would be dependent upon the response of my white cells; on occasions, I would get a reduced dose but at other times I would get no treatment to allow my healthy cells to recover.

Most importantly, this was all explained to me. At my appointment on 9 June 1977, there was no detectable disease, but I did have specific problems with my arms. I was experiencing pain in my left and right arms and on examination, my reflexes were absent in the left and reduced in the right. In addition, I had no knee-jerk reflect in my left leg.

Furthermore, I was having a strange pain, a toothache-like attack from time to time. My question was, was this a result of the drug, known to cause peripheral neuropathy and jaw pain, or was it due to active disease again? I was given no indication as to what was causing these strange manifestations; but equally, I did not ask the obvious question, was this caused by the lymphoma? My sanity would be unable to cope with the answer I dreaded more than any other.

The Vinblastine was continued at a full dose, with the period between treatments lengthened to twenty-one-day intervals. Three weeks later, I was experiencing pain and an absence of reflexes in my biceps, wrists and left triceps, plus my eyesight was becoming blurred. Dr Atkinson assured me that this was probably a result of the chemotherapy and, therefore, suggested that I have a break from treatment until these symptoms resolve.

Encouragingly, he told me that, As far as he could tell, there was no evidence of any disease. I appreciated his reassurance, but as there had been so many setbacks, my mind raced with the fear that the symptoms were due to the cancer. My anxiety reminded me that I was still terrified of a return of lymphoma.

After a few weeks without treatment, I returned to the hospital for a check-up and consideration of my future treatment management. As I sat in the waiting area, prepared for the worst but hoping for the best, my mind was occupied with questions without answers. What a relief when Dr Atkinson tells me that my blood is fine and, after a physical examination, that there were no lymph glands to be detected.

The symptoms previously reported had subsided, and I was now convinced that perhaps it had all been due to the chemotherapy. Dr Atkinson decided that the Vinblastine injections that were planned should be completed.

Of course, I had still not been privy to the knowledge that this treatment was simply palliative in nature.

Yet, even though I have the utmost of respect for the doctors, and nurses who got me through the most difficult time of my life. Everyone who nursed, and cajoled me through the real possibility of an early death — I am, however, still to this day, bewildered that there was so much collusion in respect to what was my cancer, my treatment, my future.

I simply have to accept that it was done with the best of intentions, to do otherwise would cause me to self-destruct.

Chapter 7
Heading to America

Before July 1977, I had never been fortunate enough to visit another country. But now, I had the perfect opportunity to travel to America — a long-held dream — while also taking a much-needed break to recover. Planning the trip became a welcome distraction, occupying my mind and filling me with excitement. It was a chance to step away, even briefly, from the relentless cycle of cancer treatments that had dominated my life.

Fatigue was a constant companion, a lingering reminder that my body was still fragile. For over two years, I had been trapped — first within the sterile confines of a hospital, my immune system as delicate as an eggshell, and then as an outpatient, endlessly shuttling back and forth like a yo-yo. Chemotherapy had drained me completely, stripping away every ounce of energy I once had. I often wondered — would I ever feel normal again?

But despite the exhaustion, my determination almost never wavered. America — the land of the Lakota Sioux — had captivated me for as long as I could remember. It had become more than just a fascination; it was a symbol of resilience, of survival. And now, after everything I had endured, it felt like the distant beacon that had helped me hold on to some shred of sanity.

Over the course of my illness, I had managed to save a small sum — just enough to help fund my trip. With that, I threw myself into planning; scouring newspapers and travel brochures in search of an experience that would let me see the real America. Finally, I settled on my destination: I planned to spend four weeks in North Carolina with Aunty Mary and her family.

My travel companion for this journey would be another of Mam's sisters, Aunty Kathleen. Like me, this would be her first time visiting America. Despite still feeling the lingering effects of my treatment, I hadn't given much thought to how it might impact the trip. As far as I was concerned, there would be no issues — especially since I had thoroughly discussed my plans with Dr. Atkinson. He had assured me that the holiday would do me good.

To ensure a smooth journey, he had prepared the necessary medical correspondence outlining my history. I barely gave it a second thought as I tucked the document safely into my suitcase. With the planning now complete, the long-awaited departure day had arrived. And, in late July 1977, Aunty Kathleen and I set off for North Carolina, filled with excitement and high hopes, yet carrying a quiet sense of trepidation.

As we arrived by car at Manchester Airport, my heart skipped a beat. Looming ahead, a massive jumbo jet seemed to hover above us, almost motionless as it descended. I had never truly grasped the sheer size of these machines until that moment. A rush of anxiety tightened my chest, my mouth suddenly dry. The thrill of adventure was momentarily overshadowed by the stark realization that, in mere hours, I would be soaring thousands of feet above the ground.

Fortunately, there was no time for nerves, as we were slightly behind schedule, and we needed to check in immediately. No sooner had we done this, we had to make our way into the departure lounge, and before we knew it, we were boarding the aircraft. It was all done so quickly that my anxiety was forgotten.

The entire experience felt extraordinary — my first trip abroad and a long-awaited chance to leave the shadow of cancer behind. Touching down in New York filled me with excitement, even though our journey wasn't over yet; we still had another flight to Greensboro, our final destination. However, the chaos of New York City left me unimpressed. It felt no different from any other bustling metropolis — just another crowded, noisy, and impersonal city.

Greensboro, on the other hand, was an entirely different story. As soon as the cabin door opened, I was hit by an intense wave of humidity that caught the back of my throat. The sensation was astonishing, unlike anything I had ever experienced. In that moment, I wanted to pause at the top of the stairs like a visiting head of state, waving to the unseen faces in the main building — people who had no idea of the struggles I had endured over the past two years, or what this trip truly meant to me.

Not long ago, my future had felt uncertain at best. And yet, here I was, standing on the tarmac of Greensboro Airport, thousands of miles from the world I had left behind. As we collected our bags, Aunty Mary and Uncle Jerry greeted us outside customs. Overwhelmed by the moment, I could hardly take it all in. This was more than just a journey — it was a new beginning.

Outside in the car park, Uncle Jerry's Pontiac Grand Prix gleamed under the afternoon sun — a massive, unmistakably American gas-guzzler. It was unlike anything I was used to back home. Settling into its plush seats, we rode away from the airport in style. The drive to our destination took around 45 minutes, though in my excitement, it felt like mere moments.

As we travelled through North Carolina, I couldn't help but take in my surroundings. The contrast was striking — on one side, grand, luxurious homes, many boasting sparkling swimming pools; on the other, tiny wooden huts that looked as though the slightest gust of wind might sweep them away. The extremes of wealth were unlike anything I had seen before.

Arriving at Pine Knolls in Kernersville, I was immediately taken aback by the view. The house overlooked a magnificent golf course, though the relentless summer heat had scorched the grass to a brittle brown. Stepping inside, I was greeted by a wave of cool, conditioned air. The interior was spacious and opulent, a world away from my modest home in South Shields.

Yet, despite the luxury surrounding me, I felt no envy. My illness had taught me to appreciate what I had, and I knew that money could never buy health or happiness. Our small council house back home held just as much value in my heart.

Then came the warmest welcome of all — my cousins, greeting me as though we had known each other forever. In that moment, I realized that this trip wasn't just about seeing a new place; it was about connection, about family, and about embracing life beyond illness.

Over tea, we talked for hours, covering a range of topics — not least my illness. After a while, feeling the need for some fresh air, I decided to change into a pair of shorts and take a walk around the estate. It had been so long since my legs had seen the sun, and I welcomed the warmth against my skin.

I had barely strolled a few hundred yards past the tennis courts when I heard a distinct Southern drawl: '*Take a look at that pair of skinny milk bottles!*'

I knew instantly they were referring to my pale, underexposed legs — limbs that had not only been hidden from the light for what felt like an eternity but had also borne the brutal toll of lymphoma and chemotherapy. The voices, of course, had no idea of my history. There was no malice in their words, just playful observation. I couldn't help but smile to myself — had the roles been reversed, I might have said the same thing.

My four weeks in America were nothing short of glorious, but one of the most unforgettable highlights was a trip to the Great Smoky Mountains, followed by a visit to Oconaluftee Village on the Cherokee Indian Reservation. It was the pinnacle of my trip.

As we pulled into one of the parking areas, we were immediately greeted by a Native American man — his sun-baked hand outstretched, waiting for the dollar bills that would grant tourists the privilege of taking his photograph. Sadly, he had been artificially made up for the spectacle, a representation curated for visitors rather than a true reflection of his heritage.

While there were many authentic cultural elements to admire, the sheer amount of tourist merchandise cheapened the experience somewhat. Even so, I couldn't help but be moved by the undeniable pride the Native American people held; despite the oppression and systematic injustices they had endured. Their resilience was humbling, and this visit lived up to all my expectations — a moment of deep reflection in a journey that was already so profoundly meaningful.

These resilient people had faced near annihilation at the hands of unlawful European settlers, driven by greed and avarice over centuries. And yet, their spirit remained unbroken — a strength I deeply admired and, in many ways, related to after my own battle with lymphoma.

Leaving Oconaluftee Village, we continued our journey through the Smoky Mountains. The landscape was breathtaking, a beauty so profound that mere words could never fully capture it. In a small clearing, we pulled over beside a gently gurgling stream. Without hesitation, almost instinctively, I knelt down and cupped my hands, sipping the crystal-clear, untouched water of the Oconaluftee River. It was cool, pure, and somehow felt sacred — a simple yet profound moment of connection with nature.

As we wound our way back down the mountain road, the sky darkened, and suddenly, the heavens opened. Raindrops the size of golf balls pelted the car, drumming against the roof in a deafening rhythm. Amidst the storm, I turned to Uncle Jerry and asked about visiting the Lakota tribal lands at Wounded Knee. He chuckled, shaking his head, and said, '*Pine Ridge Reservation is in South Dakota — 1,500 miles away. That's more than a 24-hour drive!*'

Still, in that moment, I silently made a promise to myself — one day, I would visit Wounded Knee and pay my respects to the proud Lakota people, who, without ever knowing it, had helped me through my own fight for survival.

During my stay in the Deep South, I met some of the warmest, most genuine people — hospitable, kind, and always ready to share a story. And they sure knew how to cook. That good old Southern food was second to none, just like the generosity of those who welcomed me into their homes.

We travelled far and saw so much — each place leaving an imprint on my heart, each moment becoming a treasured memory. But above all, it was the time spent with family that made this trip unforgettable. My cousins — Karen, David, Shelley, Scott, and Charles — helped turn these four weeks into something truly special, an experience I would carry with me forever.

One evening, Charles suggested we check out a local nightclub. Drawn by the promise of music and excitement, I eagerly agreed.

The moment we stepped inside, my English accent turned heads. It wasn't long before I caught the attention of a group of imposing Hells Angels. Clad in leather jackets, covered in tattoos, and exuding a fierce presence, they looked intimidating at first. But to my surprise, their warm smiles and enthusiasm for music quickly changed my perspective — any initial apprehension melted away.

To my amazement, these bikers turned out to be massive Hawkwind fans. Thousands of miles from home, I had somehow stumbled upon a group of space rock devotees. It was a surreal yet exhilarating moment — a reminder of how music knows no boundaries, effortlessly connecting people across continents.

We spent the night deep in conversation, swapping stories, discussing our favourite tracks, and sharing a joint as they fired off questions about Hawkwind's live performances. Most had never seen the band in concert, so I eagerly painted a picture of the hypnotic light shows, the pulsating rhythms, and the electrifying energy that defined their gigs. Their enthusiasm was infectious, making the night one I would never forget.

But the holiday wasn't just about music and camaraderie — it also held a touch of romance.

At one of the many parties thrown in my honour, I met a girl named Melissa. She had a magnetic presence, and from the moment we started talking, we were lost in conversation. We spoke of life, dreams, and everything in between, as if we had known each other forever.

As the night wound down, I walked her to her car, and in a moment that felt suspended in time, I leaned in and kissed her — a long, lingering kiss that sent a rush through me. It was spontaneous, effortless, and utterly unforgettable.

We arranged to meet the next day, and then again the day after. With each moment spent together, my feelings for Melissa deepened. She was gorgeous, captivating, and I found myself completely smitten. It felt like I was falling in love for the first time — or perhaps for the second, as I had once been just as mesmerized by the Mayor's daughter back home.

Long after I returned home, Melissa remained in my thoughts — a vivid, lingering memory of those magical, fleeting days.

Looking back, that holiday wasn't just a fun escape — it was deeply restorative. The joy, the laughter, and the connections I made had a profound impact on my health and recovery, particularly on my mental and emotional well-being. The experience felt like a turning point, reminding me of the beauty of life and the importance of embracing every opportunity.

Returning to England, I felt apprehensive about my next hospital appointment. I was feeling better than I had in months — remarkably well, in fact — but I couldn't shake the worry. Would I still feel this way after the consultation? My reflexes weren't quite as sharp as they should have been, though I hadn't noticed any real deficit, nor did I have any troubling symptoms.

With a confidence I didn't entirely feel, I waltzed into the consulting room and took my place on the examination couch. But as soon as I saw Dr. Atkinson stroll in, his usual bearded smile in place, the butterflies returned.

He asked about my trip, and I was more than happy to tell him all about it. But soon, the conversation shifted back to treatment. It had been over five weeks since my last injection, and Dr. Atkinson was keen to continue with Vinblastine therapy.

My first thought was: *When will this end?* The plan was for six more injections at two-week intervals. I could accept that — especially since Hawkwind were back on the road and heading to Newcastle in September. There was no way I was missing that. In fact, I planned to be first in the queue for tickets, and this time, I'd be taking my sister, Allyson.

Allyson was more of a David Cassidy fan — firmly in the teenybopper camp — so I had my doubts about her reaction to Hawkwind. But she knew how much the band meant to me, and she was keen to come along. After the gig, she was buzzing with excitement, almost as enthusiastic as I was. Her interest didn't last beyond that night, but it didn't matter. She had experienced the raw power of live space rock, and I had loved sharing that moment with her.

As for the proposed treatment plan, I had little choice but to accept. I had come too far to disregard medical advice now. Besides, compared to the brutal chemotherapy I had already endured, these Vinblastine injections were manageable. Any argument against them would be weak at best.

More than anything, I trusted Dr. Atkinson completely. When he explained that after the injections, I would need to be admitted to Newcastle General

Hospital for in-depth investigations to determine whether the disease was still present, I agreed without hesitation.

However, I made one thing clear: I could not — under any circumstances — be in the hospital on September 20th or October 5th. On those dates, I had two very important appointments.

The first? Newcastle City Hall.

The second? A journey to London's Hammersmith Odeon.

Both to see a certain band called Hawkwind.

There was no doubt in my mind — Hawkwind had been my lifeline through some of the darkest days of my life. Their music had carried me through so many emotional and physical struggles that I would have travelled anywhere to see them. But there was another journey I knew I had to make one day — to South Dakota and Wounded Knee. The Lakota people, without ever knowing it, had also been a source of strength, guiding me through the worst chapter of my life.

True to his word, Dr. Atkinson admitted me to Newcastle General Hospital at the end of November for a week of invasive tests — tests that would determine my future. They could bring relief or deliver a final, crushing blow.

As I stepped out of the lift onto Ward 38, I recognized many familiar faces among the nursing staff. But one face was missing — Tom, my kindred spirit, the friend who had shared my journey.

Sadly, I would never see him again.

The ward was quiet, and I was allocated a private cubicle — a stark contrast to my previous visits. That same day, they wasted no time, sending me for a bone scan and a series of X-rays. Blood samples were drawn almost daily, a routine I had long since become accustomed to.

I had driven myself up to Newcastle in my little white Hillman Imp, proudly parking it outside the hospital. From my fifth-floor window in Ward 38, I could see it below — a small but important detail, one worth remembering.

The next day, I was scheduled for a lymphangiogram. This would be my second time undergoing the procedure; the first had confirmed my diagnosis of lymphoma. In the days before CT scans, this test was the best way to assess the lymphatic system and determine whether any trace of disease remained.

Inside the treatment room, I lay back on the examination couch as the medical team prepared me. My feet were swabbed with antiseptic, the cold liquid sending a slight shiver through me. Then came the sting — local anaesthetic injected between my first two toes. Moments later, two small incisions, about an inch long, were made on the tops of my feet. Through these openings, the doctors accessed my lymphatic channels, slowly infusing a special blue contrast dye over two hours.

The dye would circulate through my lymphatic system, allowing a detailed series of X-rays to be taken — X-rays that would reveal whether the cancer still lingered in my body.

In the meantime, the contrast had some unintended but amusing side effects. For days, my urine turned bright blue, and even my skin took on a faint bluish tinge. It was a surreal reminder that my body was still a battleground, but one where I hoped the war was finally coming to an end.

After the procedure, my feet were stitched up, and I was instructed to stay in a wheelchair for at least twenty-four hours. But after the lymphangiogram investigation, in my infinite wisdom, I decided to check on my car — just to make sure it was safe and that the battery hadn't gone flat.

I manoeuvred my wheelchair into the lift, rode it down to the ground floor, and within moments, I was outside, breathing in the fresh air. Confidently, I steered my wheelchair like a Formula One driver taking on a Grand Prix circuit. The car park sloped slightly downhill — or so I thought. In reality, it was much steeper than I had realized.

At first, everything seemed under control. But as the wheelchair picked up speed, I quickly lost my grip on the situation. The momentum surged, the wheels rattled, and before I knew it, I was hurtling downhill at an alarming pace — heading straight for my pride and joy, my little car.

There was no stopping. No chance to slow down. Just one inevitable outcome.

With a thunderous crash, I slammed into the side of the vehicle. The impact jolted me, and for a brief second, I braced for the worst. But as the dust settled, I realized my biggest concern wasn't my feet, my car, or even the wheelchair. No, my real fear was that someone — anyone — had seen the entire catastrophe unfold.

Ignoring the physical pain, I could feel my face flush with embarrassment. Was someone watching from a window, barely holding back laughter? The thought made me cringe.

Luckily, everything survived the crash — my feet, the car, and the wheelchair. Only my pride had taken a serious hit. With cautious determination, I wheeled myself back up to the hospital entrance, into the lift, and back onto the ward, paranoid that someone had witnessed my stunt. No one ever admitted to seeing it. But even now, I remain convinced that some of the staff caught the spectacle and had a damn good laugh at my expense.

After all the tests were completed, I was discharged, though I still had another week to wait for the results. Seven days had never felt so long. And little did I know just how endless that wait would be.

Despite being at work during the day, my mind remained consumed by the impending test results. Surely, they had to be positive — I felt well, stronger than before. But I had felt this same optimism in the past, only to be met with crushing disappointment. Would history repeat itself?

Time dragged mercilessly, each day stretching longer than the last. Doubt crept in, uninvited but persistent. Cancer had returned so many times before, each recurrence shattering my fragile body and dismantling my mental stability. Dr. Atkinson knew how much these results meant to me. If the news was good — if I was truly free of this relentless cancer — wouldn't he have contacted me by now to end my torment?

But the silence was deafening. And as the days passed without a word, I began convincing myself that the worst was inevitable. The tests must have shown ongoing cancer. The cycle was beginning again.

Nighttime was unbearable. Sleep was a distant hope, my mind a relentless storm of uncertainty. I tossed and turned, lying awake for hours, getting up only to collapse back into bed, still unable to rest. Every night was the same, leading up to the appointment where my fate would be revealed. Exhausted but unable to quiet my thoughts, I turned to reading — Black Elk, the Lakota medicine man. But concentration eluded me. I would doze off in the chair, only to wake hours later, stiff, unrefreshed, and irritable.

The night before my appointment, the fear was overwhelming. If it was bad news, would they offer me more treatment? And even if they did — could I endure it? My body had already relapsed four times, once even during active chemotherapy. Why should this latest treatment have been any more successful than the others?

Then Thursday arrived. As always, I chose to go alone. Anxiety clawed at me as I walked into the hospital and, as usual, headed straight to the blood room for my test. The oncology clinic was just up the corridor, a short but agonizing walk away. My steps felt heavy, my gaze fixed to the ground in silent dread.

I lifted my head to see Dr Atkinson standing in the doorway.

Dr. Atkinson stood in the doorway, thirty feet away. My heart lurched; hammering so violently I thought it might burst through my chest. My mouth went dry. My hands trembled. Tears threatened to spill over as the fear gripped me tighter.

Then, suddenly, his arms shot into the air.

With a voice that filled the entire corridor, he bellowed, '*You're all clear — bloody clear!*'

Those five words were crystal clear, echoing in my mind like a stuck gramophone record. *You're all clear — bloody clear.* Even now, I hear them over and over. Had I heard him correctly? Was this real, or just a dream?

Despite the incredible news, I found myself momentarily frozen, unsure how to react. No lottery win could compare to what I had just been given. As I reached Dr. Atkinson, he took my hand and shook it firmly — with true commitment, with genuine graciousness. Emotion welled up inside me, and before I could stop them, tears rolled down my cheeks. What could I possibly say to this man — my doctor, my friend — who had just given me the greatest gift of all?

To my dying day, I will never forget that moment. Of all the suffering, the uncertainty, the relentless battle — this was the memory that would stay with me the most.

I thought back to everything that had brought me here. The aggressive, gruelling chemotherapy. The multiple relapses. The Christmas spent enduring radiotherapy that ultimately failed. And finally, the last-ditch treatment — administering a drug not to cure, but merely to manage symptoms as cancer slowly took over my body.

And yet, in the cruellest twist of irony, this so-called palliative drug had done the impossible. It had forced my cancer into remission.

I left the hospital on an artificial high, intoxicated by euphoria, desperate to share my news with the world.

That was it. Treatment was finished. I was in the clear — for now. Of course, I would need regular check-ups, and deep down, I knew I wasn't entirely out of the woods. But for the first time in years, I could focus on something other than survival.

It had been a long, brutal, emotional war against a relentless enemy. The treatment had attacked me from every possible angle, sparing no part of me — physically, mentally, and emotionally. My adolescence had been stolen, my sanity stretched to its limits. Even my body bore its scars — my testicles had shrunk to half their size due to the drugs, a cruel and humiliating legacy that would bring me untold embarrassment in the years to come. My mortality had teetered on a knife's edge more than once. The side effects had dragged me to the darkest, most punishing corners of existence — places no one should ever have to visit.

And yet, somehow, I felt grateful.

Cancer had stolen so much from me, yet, in an unexpected way, it had also given me something in return — a newfound appreciation for life. A sharper focus. A promise to myself — to live fully, to take each day as it came, to never again take time for granted. Life was too short for anything less.

But there was one regret.

I had refused to let anyone take photographs throughout my entire journey. The few that existed, I destroyed — negatives and all. At the time, the thought of preserving any visual reminder was unbearable. It was a reflex, an instinctive act of self-preservation.

Now, I wish I had them.

Paradoxically, even as I embraced life with fresh determination, part of me remained shackled to the past. My mind was a battlefield, haunted by memories I longed to discard — but couldn't. No matter how hard I tried to move forward, the echoes of my struggle lingered, refusing to fade.

For the next twelve months, I continued attending outpatient check-ups, each visit accompanied by a familiar, gnawing anxiety. No matter how well I felt, doubt would creep in, filling my mind with the same suffocating question: What if the lymphoma is back?

The uncertainty was relentless. Would they confirm I was still clear? Or would there be hesitation in their voices, leading to more tests, more waiting, more fear? Each time, I braced for the worst. And yet, each time, I received the only answer that mattered — no signs of cancer.

Between hospital visits, I found solace in music. Seeing Hawkwind live once again rekindled the inspiration and positive energy they had given me during my darkest days. Their music transported me, lifting my spirit and reminding me of the strength I had found within myself.

By the end of 1978, I returned to America — this time to Tennessee, where Aunty Mary and Uncle Jerry had moved. Once again, I found myself drawn to the Smoky Mountains, to Oconaluftee Village, and to the mystical Cherokee people. But more than anything, it was the Lakota Sioux and Wounded Knee that called to me. There was something there — something I needed to understand, to connect with.

For a time, I even considered leaving England altogether, setting up a new life in America, far from the ghosts of my illness. A fresh start — a chance to rebuild. But fate had other plans. Moving across the Atlantic was not to be my path.

My mind was a constant battleground, swinging between the extremes of deep, unshakable melancholy and bursts of euphoria. The uncertainty about my future gnawed at me, filling me with doubt and confusion. I couldn't make sense of my emotions — flashes of fear, trepidation, and an inexplicable turmoil that I neither understood nor controlled.

The chaos inside me took its toll. I even missed the final home game of the season — a thrilling 3-0 defeat of Burnley — something I never would have imagined skipping.

And still, the intrusive, tormenting thoughts persisted. Day after day — hour after hour. A relentless presence that refused to let me go.

Chapter 8
The Joys of Parenthood

Illness has woven itself into the very fabric of my life, at times becoming all-consuming and causing me to miss out on so much that others took for granted. Whenever I finally had the chance to get out, I travelled the length and breadth of the country to see Hawkwind. For me, this was more than just a concert; it was a way to repay the support they had unknowingly offered during my darkest hours.

Throughout my youth, they kept me focused and grounded, just as the resilient people of the great Sioux Empire had. Yet, despite their support, I couldn't shake the feeling that much of my adolescence had been stripped away without my consent. How could I ever call my cancer experience '*normal*'? Though it was anything but, that experience shaped my belief system, creating a pathway marked by both innocence and guilt. I was a survivor, but survivorship brought its own set of challenges — my shadow and I became constant companions.

As the 1970s drew to a close, while many of my friends were busy planning their weddings, I could count on one hand the girlfriends I had known — all of them before my illness. I felt an intense desire to settle down, to marry, and to fit into the mould society expected of me. But that decision would lead to heartache; my first marriage was fraught with conflict, ultimately ending in divorce. Still, it was a journey filled with moments of joy and deep despair as a father. Like many broken marriages, I had to confront my part in its failure.

In 1979, I met my first wife. Looking back, it's clear that our union was a knee-jerk reaction to my longing for what I perceived as '*being normal.*' For so long, cancer had restricted my ability to experience life like everyone else, and I yearned to finally embrace what I believed was a '*normal' existence.* Yet, the reality was far more complex, filled with lessons learned in both love and loss.

Not only did I miss out on so much of my adolescence, but I also skipped the journey of discovery that comes with exploring relationships with the opposite sex. In time, I found a girlfriend — an only child, spoiled by her aging parents. Unfortunately, she turned out to be a very jealous woman, despite my insistence that she had nothing to fear. I can say, hand on heart, that during our troubled marriage, I never once gave her a reason for her jealousy. Yet, as the years passed, I faced baseless accusations of affairs with nurses, my best friend's wife, and even other men — none of which had any substance or truth.

While I don't want to dwell on past mistakes, it's important to acknowledge how the hasty decisions I made due to my illness had dire consequences that affected not just me, but many lives. The harsh reality of my cancer diagnosis loomed over our marriage like a dark cloud, reminding us that the final whistle of such a diagnosis never truly blows.

In the beginning, despite the challenges, things seemed to be okay. We both shared a desire to start a family, believing that life wouldn't feel complete without children. We agreed that having at least two children would be ideal. However, as time passed, it became increasingly clear that nothing was happening.

After six months of trying, we felt the urge to seek help from a doctor, wondering if the issue lay with her or with me — or if perhaps we simply hadn't given it enough time. Having moved away from my previous doctor's practice after getting married, we scheduled an appointment with our family doctor.

He seemed noticeably nervous when we broached the subject of our struggle to conceive. His discomfort was palpable as he shifted in his seat, and then he delivered the heart-wrenching news: because of the type of chemotherapy I had undergone years earlier, it was unlikely that I would ever be able to father children. In that moment, the weight of my past decisions came crashing down, leaving us both reeling from the implications.

I was left stunned and speechless. No one had ever approached this scenario before, and I couldn't recall any healthcare professional even hinting that infertility might be a possibility. I felt gutted, tearful, and filled with a sense of outrage — I felt cheated and abused. After surviving the horrendous experience of cancer and enduring its debilitating treatment, this felt like yet another assault. I couldn't help but wonder if my ordeal with cancer would ever truly come to an end.

Cancer doesn't just stop influencing your life once treatment is completed; it continued to cast a long shadow over mine. And believe me, I was furious. In retrospect, I found myself angrier with the medical profession than with the disease itself. The cancer could have taken my life, yet here I was, having survived against all odds, now grappling with the painful aftermath. I had developed a healthy respect for this unforgiving condition, but I was left feeling betrayed by those who had treated me.

The doctors must have known that the treatment would lead to infertility, yet they had failed to inform me. Perhaps they never expected me to survive at all. Alongside my own turmoil, I felt a heavy burden of guilt for my wife. She was now left to wrestle with this unfortunate situation, struggling to cope through no fault of her own.

Yes, I was free from the dreaded malignancy, and I was grateful for that, but the bitter aftertaste of infertility dulled my anticipation and determination to become a parent. A couple of months later, however, we made a decision: we would not be beaten by this challenge. We would seek a different path — adoption. In that moment, hope began to flicker anew, as we set out on a journey to build a family in a way we had never imagined.

Unfortunately, the journey to adoption was not as easy as we had hoped. After reaching out to several local adoption agencies, we were met with swift rejections, often without any explanation. Even the local social services determined that my cancer history made me unfit to be considered as a prospective adoptive parent.

Ironically, the fostering and adoption officer who had previously declined our application went on to have a baby herself. However, a new social worker named Maggie took over and began reviewing old files. To my surprise, she discovered ours and later confessed to being bewildered by our initial rejection. She reached out to us, asking if she could come for a visit. This meeting marked not only the start of a professional relationship but also the beginning of a great friendship.

Maggie explained that there was no reason we couldn't start by fostering children, with the hope of moving toward long-term fostering and eventually adoption. She agreed to set the process in motion, outlining that we would need to complete references and police checks as part of the system.

In less than six months, after countless interviews and assessments, we found ourselves before a matching panel, hopeful to be considered for a fostering position with a child currently in short-term placement. Her name was Donna. Maggie explained that Donna needed long-term stability, and she believed we were the right people to provide it. With that, a glimmer of hope began to emerge as we stepped into this new chapter of our lives, eager to embrace the opportunity to nurture and care for a child in need.

We agreed immediately, and plans were soon made for our first meeting with Donna. To say I was filled with trepidation in the hours leading up to our rendezvous at her short-term foster home would be an understatement. When we arrived, we were ushered into the foster parents' front room, where the foster Mam brought Donna downstairs.

What a little picture, what a beautiful girl she was — a two-year-old with large, brown, hypnotic eyes and a beauty that radiated innocence. However, there was no smile on her face. Her mousy, shoulder-length hair hung freely, and she wore a simple blue pinafore dress. As I reached out, Donna kept her distance, hesitant to come near me. We spent an hour together, but after that first visit, we left with a quiet understanding to return the following evening.

When we returned, something had shifted. Donna seemed to almost forget her earlier fear. She approached me, holding one of her toys, and tilted her head slightly, offering the faintest hint of a smile. That small gesture meant the world to me; it signified acceptance and connection after such a short time. In that moment, my heart swelled with hope, and I knew we were taking the first steps toward building a bond that could blossom into something beautiful.

Donna had been moved so many times in her short life that she was overly friendly towards strangers, as if instinctively aware that another change was always on the horizon. At just two-years-old, I believed she sensed that yet another move was imminent, a heart-wrenching reality for a child so young.

It was agreed that the sooner Donna could move in with us, the better we could begin to establish a bond. I will never forget the day we collected her, leaving behind that house with her meagre possessions crammed into a brown paper carrier bag. It was a beautiful summer Saturday afternoon, and as we drove home, a mix of excitement and apprehension filled the air. We knew this would be a challenging time for her, so we planned to keep her occupied and engaged.

Once we arrived, our focus was entirely on Donna. Lunch was first on the agenda, and we followed it up with chocolate pudding — a sweet treat that would undoubtedly bring some joy. Every father imagines moments like these, capturing the essence of childhood in all its messy glory. True to form, Donna was soon covered in pudding, her infectious smile beaming from ear to ear. That delightful mess made for a perfect photograph, a snapshot of a beautiful beginning as we embarked on this journey together.

She had enjoyed a lovely afternoon, but as evening fell, exhaustion took over, and she drifted into sleep on the couch. However, when we gently placed her into her new bed, she awoke abruptly, her cries piercing the silence. From that night onward, her inconsolable tears became indelibly imprinted in my mind.

Night after night, she would sob herself to sleep, and for a long time, there was little we could do to comfort her.

Despite these difficult nights, life was now about cherishing Donna and the happiness she brought into our home. She was a joy, filling our days with laughter and love. Though she was slow in her psychological development — something the health visitor attributed to her frequent relocations — we were unconcerned. She was with us, and that was all that mattered. For the first time in a long while, life seemed to be settling into something close to normal.

But if I had learned anything, it was that normal never lasted for long.

In 1984, without warning, my own health took a sudden and terrifying turn. The night sweats returned, a relentless fatigue set in, and within days, I was too weak to get out of bed. What started as an unexplained illness quickly spiralled, leaving me bedridden for a week. When I began drifting in and out of consciousness, my family called an emergency doctor. After a brief examination, he wasted no time — he picked up the phone and called for an ambulance.

Late that night, I was admitted to Sunderland Royal Hospital.

The following days passed in a blur of tests and procedures — scans, bloodwork, even a lumbar puncture. The doctors initially suspected cancer, a word that sent a familiar chill down my spine. I had been through this before; I knew the drill. But I also knew my body. There were no lumps, no obvious signs of malignancy. Eventually, after exhaustive investigations, the diagnosis came back: a severe viral infection.

Relief should have washed over me, but the reality of living with a past cancer diagnosis is that it never truly leaves you. Every unexplained symptom, every cough, every fever feels like the beginning of something worse. The fear lingers, always waiting in the shadows.

I don't believe this was a case of paranoia — it was an entirely natural reflex. A fear that cancer might once again take hold of my life, threatening my very existence. Logically, I understood that just because I had battled cancer once didn't mean every illness signalled its return. Like anyone else, I was susceptible to colds, aches, and the usual ailments of life. The challenge was learning to rationalize these fears, to put them into perspective.

As I've mentioned before, cancer doesn't simply loosen its grip once treatment ends. Even when remission is declared, its shadow lingers, shaping how you see the world. One of the strangest lingering effects for me was tied to Vincristine, a chemotherapy drug that left an indelible mark on my senses. I still remember the peculiar taste it triggered the moment it entered my veins, an artificial, almost metallic tang that no drink could mask. I would sip orange juice in an attempt to drown it out, but it was futile. Worse still, the drug played tricks on my sense of smell, creating an association so powerful that it would come back to haunt me years later.

It was five years after completing my chemotherapy, on what should have been an ordinary summer day. I was walking along a quiet country path, the warm breeze carrying the scent of wildflowers and fresh earth. Then, without warning, a nauseating smell filled my nostrils — one I hadn't encountered in years but recognized instantly.

Vincristine!

The mere scent sent a wave of sickness through me, as if I had been transported back to those gruelling treatment days. But where was it coming from? I searched for the source, and soon I found it — a cluster of Rosebay Willow, commonly known as fireweed or bomb weed, its pink blooms scattered across the countryside.

It was a cruel twist of fate. That seemingly innocuous plant carried the exact scent of the drug that had once coursed through my fragile veins, reviving not only the smell but the unbearable taste and nausea that had accompanied it.

Even years later, cancer had a way of finding me, reminding me of its presence in the most unexpected ways.

My senses were thrown into turmoil, my psyche unsettled, as this unexpected phenomenon stirred something deep within me. The scent alone was enough to awaken my darkest thoughts, reigniting fears I had long tried to suppress. A wave of nausea swept over me, mirroring the sickening side effects of chemotherapy as if no time had passed at all.

I was bewildered by the power of this memory — how a simple smell could transport me so forcefully back to a place I never wanted to revisit. From that moment on, I made a conscious effort to avoid any contact with fireweed, steering clear of its presence whenever I could.

Because once you've been touched by cancer, its shadow never truly fades. It lingers, a lifelong legacy that follows you, waiting to resurface when you least expect it.

Chapter 9
The Words that All Parents Fear

In 1985, the year 'Live Aid' took place at Wembley and almost a year and a half since Donna, four-years-old, became an invaluable member of the family, things appeared to be going as they should, or so I thought. It was a normal Saturday morning, plans for breakfast together and then a ride into town.

However, this particular morning turned out to be far from normal when I discovered a lump the size of a walnut on Donna's left elbow, which certainly hadn't been there previously. Naturally concerned, I hurriedly got myself and then Donna dressed and headed straight down to the doctor. Nothing to worry about, a simple infection in her arm, antibiotics will sort it out, was his response.

Donna was otherwise well and, therefore, I had no reason to doubt him, so I left the surgery, collected the antibiotics, and then headed off home. Seven days later, having completed the treatment, the lump was still there, completely unchanged, so we went back to the doctors.

He sat in his chair and confidently stated, '*She simply hasn't responded to the antibiotics, we'll give her a different prescription.*'

He had examined Donna and found a small lump in her neck too, clear evidence in his view that this was an infection. Despite being dubious regarding his diagnosis, I had never had any problems with him previously and so I, again, accepted his explanation and headed off to the chemist to collect the next antibiotics.

Less than a week later, there was no change. This time, I took Donna straight to the Accident and Emergency department to see a Paediatrician, but even there the on-call doctor was quite dismissive of my concerns. As if to appease my nagging persistence, a blood test was taken and showed marginal anaemia and an elevation of her white cell count, which potentially could go hand in hand with an infection.

However, as far as the doctor was concerned, this was nothing to worry about. But, considering these findings, we were asked to arrange an appointment the following Monday in the children's ward in Sunderland Royal Hospital. I knew from my experience of illness that an elevated white count can be seen in several infective states but, of course, it could also be the first indication of something more sinister.

As such, I felt it warranted further investigation; particularly as Donna had already had antibiotics for fourteen days without any response. As requested, Donna attended the children's ward on Monday and had various tests done during that week, including a biopsy of the lump on her arm that was causing so much of my concern. Despite all the investigations, she ran around the ward like an Olympic athlete.

The Consultant in his infinite wisdom decided that this was sufficient proof that Donna was a healthy fit child, seemingly basing his diagnosis on this fact alone and she was subsequently discharged home with no specific medical condition being detected. Instead, the Consultant declared that she would be as *'right as rain'* in no time.

Having no experience of health care apart from my illness, I felt ill-equipped to challenge his decision. So, I did exactly as he asked; I took Donna home, expecting her to resume normal activity. If the Consultant felt there was little to be concerned about, then who was I to question that expertise?

In the middle of the following week, whilst at work, I received a phone call from the hospital asking my wife and me to attend to discuss Donna's test results. I distinctly remember driving from Wallsend to Sunderland thinking it must be something serious, but never in my wildest dreams did I have any suspicion of what was about to be disclosed.

My wife had already made her way to the hospital. We met in the corridor and hurried along to the ward, where the ward sister greeted us as if she had been expecting our arrival — directing us to two chairs placed regimentally outside the Consultant's office. During our wait, sitting there patiently, the dulcet tone of the Consultant could be heard, instructing the nursing Sister, *'Get some tea and stay in whilst I speak to these parents.'*

Hearing his orders, made me suspicious, and I became concerned as to what he was about to tell us; my heart began to thump loudly, and my mouth became dry as if stuffed full of cotton wool. My concern was well-founded as you could have knocked me over with a feather when the Consultant blurted out immediately when we entered the room, without any compassion or hesitation, *'What do you know about Lymphoma?'*

After a moment's pause, I responded, *'Are you saying Donna has Lymphoma?'*

His response was short and seemed to be lacking any empathy, '*Yes,*' he replied, '*sister will tell you more,*' and then marched out of the office.

This devastating news left us both numb with shock; the tingling pain of emotion was overwhelming. We were lost for words whilst our world was collapsing around us. It was so difficult to comprehend and what angered me more than anything else was that, eventually, against all the odds, we now had the chance to share our lives with a bundle of joy, Donna. Yet, she was about to face the same life-threatening scenario that I had faced less than ten years earlier.

Her future was now uncertain; having to endure the same debilitating treatment I had received, the same treatment that had come close to destroying me not just physically, but also mentally.

The main centre for paediatric Oncology was based in Newcastle, and we were told to report to Ward 16 South, at the Royal Victoria Infirmary, the following day.

We were so confused and upset when we arrived back home, not knowing whom to tell first or even if we should tell anyone at this early stage. We hoped that perhaps once we got to Newcastle, it would prove to be something much more innocent and not lymphoma, but was this just grasping at straws, or would my hope be justified?

Remember, our family doctor told us that Donna had nothing more than an infection and the Consultant of Paediatrics, at Sunderland, informed us that Donna was fine and too lively to be significantly poorly; we could only hope that both were right in that conclusion after all.

Donna had no symptoms apart from a few swollen lymph nodes and was indeed well. I suppose deep down my understanding of lymphoma told me that these were not innocent swellings. But, in reality, I wanted to avoid believing that, and I had to have hope. We travelled to Newcastle the next morning, reaching the Royal Victoria Infirmary shortly after the rush hour.

We entered the hospital and made our way along what felt like an endless, green-tiled Victorian corridor, eventually, arriving at the oncology ward where we were greeted by the stench of antiseptic, which created a noticeable fear in the pit of my stomach. What's more, some children were lying on their beds; others were running around the ward and many of them had no hair, a clear reminder as to why they were there and the treatment they had recently endured.

We were greeted by Liz, a young staff nurse, who became a good friend and confidante during the forthcoming weeks and months. There was little doubt that despite the seriousness of the conditions of the children here, the ward had a wonderful feeling to it, friendly and relaxed. Our first meeting with the Consultant compounded our heartache as a diagnosis for Donna was not as clear-cut as we had been led to believe, and she would require further investigations.

Yes, she did indeed have a lymphoma; however, the specific type was unclear and clarity was essential as different lymphomas require different treatment approaches. One thing was certain; this was indeed a malignancy, a cancer, and a real threat to the life of our little girl. The biopsy had confirmed that diagnosis.

In those early days when blood was required, and it was often daily, Donna simply offered her arm, ready for the removal of the red substance. But, it would not take too long before she learned that cooperation was not a requisite. She quickly figured out that she did not have to give her consent freely, or volunteer herself for tests, that on the surface may appear innocent.

Donna very soon became suspicious of any member of staff who approached her, and it became a battle — a psychological battle. But at other times it would be a physical battle to retrieve the required samples, or to persuade Donna to leave the ward for some investigation. Understandably, she could not comprehend the rationale for all, or indeed any of these tests.

Whenever a nurse or doctor came to her bedside, she would compassionately look into my eyes as if seeking protection. My concern was that this situation would challenge our relationship; naturally, she was expecting me, her father, to stop these interventions from taking place but, clearly, I couldn't do that.

I was not aware at the time, but her cancer was in her bone marrow and the malignant cells were overcrowding this important space to such an extent that her healthy cells were unable to function or re-populate. Subsequently, Donna would require blood and platelet transfusions regularly.

One of the necessary tests was a repeated tissue biopsy, this time the enlarged lymph node in Donna's neck was to be excised and sent for analysis, and it needed to be done in theatre under a general anaesthetic.

Anyone who has escorted his or her child to a theatre in readiness for an operation knows the fear and anxiety that runs through your body as you make the long journey down the busy corridor. The nurse running alongside the trolley trying her best to make Donna smile but failing miserably as she understood something quite unpleasant was about to happen.

After what seemed a half-marathon around the hospital, we finally arrived at the theatre and the fear really started to kick in. I had already been unable to convince myself that she was in safe hands and doubt entered my mind, a thousand confused fears suggesting to my unconscious mind that something may go wrong.

I felt overwhelmed by the silent screams trying to escape from inside my head, the pounding sound of each beat of my heart, and the distinct dryness inside my mouth. Not only that, but I tried to put on a brave face for Donna. She held on tightly to Lolly Lodle, the name she had given to her favourite doll. All too soon, it was time to let the anaesthetist do her job, but a gigantic lump stuck in my throat. A noxious sinking feeling consumed me when the theatre assistant recommended that we return to the ward once the fairy wind had taken effect, and Donna had drifted into an artificial sleep.

Some hour and a half later and Donna was returned safely to the ward and slept for the next hour. Frustratingly, it was now time to play the waiting game, what exactly would the biopsy show? Not surprisingly, Donna made a full recovery from the theatre experience, waking with an infectious smile, causing my tears to once again roll down my cheeks.

Sometime later that week, Donna was about to start some chemotherapy as a high-grade, Non-Hodgkin lymphoma had been diagnosed which required immediate treatment to prevent further advancement. The nightmare was about to commence, reliving and confronting my fears concerning chemotherapy, I knew exactly what this chemotherapy was capable of, and I worried about Donna's ability to cope with this difficult treatment.

My feelings of apprehension and emotional instability were matched only by the fear I felt watching Donna receive chemotherapy drugs similar to those I'd received less than ten years previous. I struggled to accept the helplessness of seeing Donna undergo this chemotherapy and to deal with all the memories it elicited for me.

I felt completely useless, not being able to protect my little girl, or have the treatment in her place. Indeed, it was harder watching Donna receive the treatment than it was to experience a similar, painful voyage myself, and that had been an almighty struggle. Yet, I would have happily accepted the entire nightmare again if it had relieved the need for Donna to be put through that torment.

Strangely and in many respects, Donna made life as easy as it could have been in that unenviable position, her smile and lovable character, her innocence, and her trust in us as parents made that intolerable situation so much easier. If Donna coped, how could we as parents not? At times, it felt as if Donna was supporting us rather than the other way around.

From the very moment that you take your first tentative steps on the road of a cancer pathway, every day tends to merge into one and time is of little consequence any more. The only thing that is of any importance is helping and supporting your child cope with what to them is an unknown experience.

You simply cannot explain to a three-year-old the full implications of a cancer diagnosis, and particularly, what the consequences of that diagnosis might be. That kaleidoscope of emotional turbulence returns, and the roller-coast ride of unprecedented emotions firmly positions your sanity on the edge of time. Once on that roller coaster ride, it's difficult to stop the ride and get off.

It was all about to begin again, just as it did back in 1975, but this time I had far more understanding of the predicament and all of its implications, many of which I had simply not wanted to confront. However, this time there was no question of not being strong or not being able to cope, as I now had parental responsibility and an unswerving obligation to Donna.

Many discussions took place with both the medical and nursing fraternity, who had a wealth of experience in respect to helping parents address these extremely difficult situations. Many people may believe that a child has a right to know what is going on and attempts should be made to explain the meaning of a condition such as cancer.

However, many parents again will disagree and prefer to cushion their children from such exposure. Neither approach is correct, yet, neither is wrong. The correct choice has to be the one that is right for your child as you, the parent, see it. Once you make that decision, no one can criticize it.

As parents, we decided that we would explain to Donna as best we could about this dreaded condition. The most feared diagnosis known to society, a diagnosis that not everyone survives, although we wanted to avoid confronting that part of the brittle equation.

The mutual support from other parents we met at the hospital was incredible, and it was a fact that you could not get through the nightmare without that support. Donna was fitted with a special device called a Hickman line that allowed the chemotherapy to be administered, blood to be taken and most importantly avoided the need for further needles to be stuck into her fragile veins.

The device has revolutionized modern-day chemotherapy, particularly for children. But even this marvellous device, didn't ease my feeling of helplessness at being unable to take away Donna's pain and sickness as only a father should. Donna soon lost her hair, but this really didn't bother her as much as it bothered us.

We found it offensive and hurtful when ignorant people would stand and blatantly stare when Donna walked past, clearly bald as a result of the unforgiving treatment; thankfully, she seemed unaware of their behaviour. Losing her hair was also a constant reminder to us of the seriousness of her current cancer and the threat to her life.

Donna was supplied with a brown wig and at every opportunity, she would proudly wear this. At times, however, when she was hot or eating something that needed her utmost concentration, it would be whipped off with a flick of her right wrist, often to the surprise of unsuspecting passers-by.

On one occasion between treatments, we had travelled to Blackpool, one of Donna's favourite destinations. During the visit, Donna had asked for candy floss and while she was eating this, the wind began to blow, causing hair from her wig to get in her mouth.

Undaunted, she simply put one hand on the top of her head, and with one quick tug, the wig was removed with impish nonchalance. She continued to devour the candy floss, the whole action having taken less than a couple of seconds. However, just at that moment, a gentleman was passing by, and his bottom lip dropped almost to his feet as he observed Donna's actions.

As Hawkwind, and the Lakota people, had been such an inspiration to me, I couldn't help but wonder if Hawkwind's music could help Donna. It turned out that she didn't like the majority of their music. However, there were nights when Donna went to bed when I would sit at the bottom of her bed and play some of the more ambient Hawkwind tracks as she fell asleep. I particularly remember playing a number called '*Wind of Change*,' and ironically, one of my favourites.

Over the next couple of months, Donna got weaker and weaker and picked up one infection after another, which required many hospital admissions for intravenous antibiotics. Indeed, she had her fourth birthday in hospital. Donna was given some time off the treatment in an attempt to increase her weight, and generally get stronger. But, there was a need to weigh up the risk of stopping the treatment against the benefits of waiting to see if she improved.

However, after only two weeks, the team at Newcastle felt that it was important to recommence the chemotherapy as this cancer could not be left untreated. Sadly, following this treatment Donna appeared to suffer worse side effects than previously; a sickness that threatened to turn her stomach inside out and lethargy, leaving her bereft of motivation and an absence of her hypnotic smile.

With no desire to eat and incapable of moving from her bed, she was deteriorating in front of our eyes. There is no known coping strategy a parent can elicit when a child is struck by such an aggressive disease and, therefore, I cannot even attempt to explain how we as parents got through that impossible situation.

Make no mistake about it; the real coping mechanism was Donna! Despite her illness and suffering, she made things so much easier for us. Even though she was so poorly, Donna was a rock and made us feel very humble, as did all the children who were also with her on the same reluctant journey. With Donna so stoical, how on earth could we crumble in front of her?

Once at home, however, our emotions would fall to pieces like large chunks of ice falling from a glacier. My heart was breaking, and at times I felt like an inconsolable wreck, and I could not see an end to this nightmare. Donna's Mam suffered the same emotional turmoil, and helplessness, in the same way, which I did. Mutually, we felt Donna's pain, yet together, we were unable to ease that suffering.

Yet as a parent, nothing but nothing can prepare you for the assault and battery inflicted by an unseen condition that affects every part of your person. But somewhere inside, you have just got to find the bravery and courage that is needed to support your child. Ultimately, you never lose sight of the determination, the focus that your child will get better.

Yes, there are times when you doubt that, but even then, you must convince yourself that one day the nightmare will end, if you don't, you'll lose your mind. On 22 August 1985, we were back in hospital at Newcastle for further treatment and things did not appear to be going to plan.

Donna was now so weak that I had to carry her from the car to the ward. The treatment itself was not having the desired effect against this vicious cancer and, therefore, further investigations were requested by Dr Craft, including a lumbar puncture. Donna appeared to be slipping away, losing her ability to live, her feeble frame now lying still on the bed, any movement causing her pain and upset.

Later in the evening, we were asked to go into the office with the Consultant.

It was obvious by his demeanour that this was serious, '*We do not think Donna can take any more chemotherapy,*' he said.

When I asked about the implication of this, he said with heartfelt compassion, '*I'm afraid there is no more we can do for Donna.*'

On hearing the words that each, and every parent fears, the words you never want to be spoken. I have no shame in admitting that I just broke down and cried. My entire body was numb with shock, my mind was attacked by fear and no one was able to take away that unrivalled heartache, no one able to ease this unbearable nightmare, my entire system tingling with shock and disbelief.

Not knowing what to do, what to say, and how to react to an impossible situation. Eventually, as I sobbed, I recall asking Dr. Craft the question that I didn't want an answer to, '*How long does she have*?'

That is a question that just cannot be answered with any accuracy, but what he said, hit me like a brick wall in the face. '*She may go during the night, it could be days or weeks, she is very poorly at present.*'

The feeling this news elicits is, undoubtedly, indescribable. Apparently, this was not a lymphoma after all. They suggested that what Donna had was an extremely rare form of adult cancer, called Chronic Myeloid Leukaemia, and there was no available treatment other than to keep her comfortable.

Donna was moved into a side room and we both stayed with her that night, and it was an emotional tornado that I feared would sweep away my sanity. Donna was almost unresponsive in her consciousness, requiring lots of medication to keep her comfortable, yet despite my worst fears, Donna did survive that night and the next and the next.

The Consultant still felt that she would die soon and as a family, we were living on borrowed time. With such impending doom, I had to try to think logically. My little girl had been passed from pillar to post throughout her short life, known no consistency and according to the doctors, she was dying.

The main concern of my wife was that Donna had never been christened and even though the decision was not legally ours to make, we did exactly that and Donna was christened in the chapel at the Royal Victoria Infirmary. The Charge Nurse, Steve, was her Godfather and Liz, her named nurse, was her Godmother.

Afterward, back on the ward, the staff had laid on a party for Donna and the other children. That was a unique day indeed, and although Donna simply lay on her bed throughout the proceedings as she was so fragile. She still managed to smile as the other kids, and parents, all tried to ensure that Donna was the centre of attention.

The paradox of the situation wasn't lost on me; we were in the midst of a christening party for Donna, yet we were struggling to cope with the knowledge and persecution of the reality of losing our precious daughter. It remains the hardest concept to explain, you are told that your innocent child is going to die, yet as you watch her from a distance, it is impossible to believe, impossible to accept and even more impossible to understand.

How can you come to terms with this frightening dilemma? Quite simply, I do not believe you can. You can try to appease yourself that your child will be going to a better place if indeed you believe in a better place. But irrespective, there is still a considerable void, a chasm waiting to engulf the rest of your life.

You can try to put it out of your mind, but quite honestly, we found that was almost impossible. Donna retained such a cheery disposition which made the whole process so surreal and strangely and ironically, it seemed that once again, Donna was actually supporting us, through the nightmare no one wants to enter.

No matter what your belief systems are, I do not believe any coping mechanisms can prepare you for the death of a child. With no treatment offered, the only plan was to keep Donna comfortable with blood and platelet transfusions whenever they were required.

This went on for almost ten days, after which time Donna was stronger than she had been in quite some weeks; strong enough to return home, assuming that we brought her back each day for monitoring. The uncontrollable need and necessity to remain positive day in and day out in the hope that Donna would remain well became an exhausting occupation.

Talking with other parents in the same predicament as us, they would profess to be positive of mind, but admitted that it was hard work convincing oneself to remain positive. Within the seclusion and confines of your home, with the time to reflect on the cancer that was engulfing your child, and consuming your life, that positive attitude would very often evaporate. Then, seeds of doubt would typically become an overpowering burden.

Interestingly, some months later, completely unexpectedly, Donna spoke about the night she nearly died. She claimed to recall floating above her bed and seeing both her Mam and Dad crying and seeing a tunnel with the most unusual pretty bright lights at the end. She then claimed that a voice told her, *'It's not your time, go back to your Mam and Dad.'*

I'm sure many will pour scorn on this so-called out-of-body experience or this near-death experience, call it what you will. But this was from the mouth of a four-year-old and without any prompts. Even today, we know so little about life itself, especially the mind.

Of course, stories such as these are not uncommon but do lead to compounding what is a complex, but fascinating issue. Whether this is the mind playing games, our inner psyche, or something else is not open for debate here, but whatever it is, it is a fascinating discussion for another day. Little did I know that soon, I would receive the most unexpected news.

Chapter 10
Like Father, Like Daughter

Once Donna was back at home, one of the first things that I would arrange, something I should have done months earlier, was to start Donna on a daily dose of Ginseng. Was I grasping at straws? Almost certainly yes, but who knows what significance it played in my recovery, perhaps none, but it could have been one of a handful of significant ingredients in my successful recovery from my cancer diagnosis.

Irrespective of whether it had played any part in my recovery or not, what was important was that it certainly did no harm. Therefore, I went out and bought some Ginseng for Donna, and she remained on the herb for many months, taking the elixir each morning without fail. Although it was harmless, it's not recommended to take it continuously, so she was given Ginseng for a month and then had a month's rest before starting again.

As Donna loved Blackpool, we planned to spend all the time we had left with her, going there as often as possible. Initially, following the terminal prognosis, we had decided to visit Disneyland in Florida, but we were advised against taking Donna out of the country because of her fragile condition. The risk of infection or the potential for her health to rapidly decline was too great. Not to mention that medical insurance would not have been possible to secure.

Another concern weighing on me was work. I had been granted a leave of absence due to Donna's deterioration, but what about the long term? With so much uncertainty surrounding Donna's very existence, I felt unable to return to work. As a result, I asked my employer if I could take voluntary redundancy — a request they tentatively agreed to consider.

Looking back, I realize my decision may have been a knee-jerk reaction. If Donna passed away, as the hospital had predicted, it would undoubtedly be an emotionally devastating time. However, at some point, I would still need to return to work. This dilemma only deepened my confusion about the best course of action, but at that moment, my priority was clear — I wanted the freedom to spend as much time with Donna as possible.

In situations like this, logic often takes a backseat, which is likely why management chose to take some time before responding to my request. Less than a week later, my manager asked me to come in at my earliest convenience to discuss the matter further.

During our meeting, he acknowledged the difficulty of my circumstances and kindly offered to keep my position open indefinitely if I wished to extend my leave. However, my mind was made up. Accepting redundancy would provide the extra financial support I needed to do the things that mattered most to Donna. And so, I chose that path.

As far as I was concerned, this decision would allow me to fulfil Donna's wishes without the added worry of finances. Once again, fate seemed to be playing a significant role in my life.

Like so many others, Donna was a huge wrestling fan. At the time, Big Daddy (Shirley Crabtree) and Giant Haystacks were at the height of their fame. Donna absolutely adored Big Daddy — so imagine our surprise when, as we drove into Blackpool, we saw a poster emblazoned with the words: '*Professional Wrestling Tonight.*' And, as if it were meant to be, guess who was set to appear in the ring? None other than, '*Big Daddy,*' himself.

It felt like an incredible stroke of luck, or fate. Once we were settled into our hotel, my first priority was to secure tickets for the show. But I wanted to do something even more special for Donna. I decided to track down Big Daddy's manager, which, to my surprise, wasn't too difficult. When I found him, I explained why we were there and asked if there was any chance Donna could meet her hero. Without hesitation, he assured me it wouldn't be a problem and told us to wait in the corner of the hall after the show.

As expected, *Big Daddy* won his match to thunderous applause. When the hall had emptied, we made our way to the designated corner as instructed. Moments later, Big Daddy emerged and warmly invited us back to his changing room.

He was an absolute diamond — gracious, kind, and a true gentleman. But most importantly, he was fantastic with Donna. He spoke to her with such warmth, even telling her that '*she was one of his heroes.*'

It was an incredibly emotional moment — there wasn't a dry eye in the house. Knowing that Donna's life expectancy was limited, yet seeing her so happy and content in the presence of one of her heroes, was truly wonderful. As we made our way back to the hotel, all we heard about was '*Big Daddy*' — '*Big Daddy*' this, '*Big Daddy*' that. She was absolutely over the moon.

The following day, we returned to the North East with Donna still riding the high of her unforgettable experience, proudly wearing her *'Big Daddy'* hat and scarf. Back at the hospital, she couldn't wait to tell everyone about her special friend. The nurses listened intently as she enthusiastically recounted how *'Big Daddy'* had defeated his arch-rival, *'Giant Haystacks.'* The joy and pride in her voice was infectious.

After the Consultant examined Donna and conducted the usual blood tests, she was given a platelet transfusion. Other than that, the medical team was pleased with her condition — there was no need for any further intervention. With this reassurance, and with Donna still in high spirits, we decided to return to Blackpool just a day later.

It was almost as if Donna had transformed into a different person. Just weeks earlier, she had been weak, helpless, and in constant discomfort. Now, she was full of energy, engaged, and enjoying life. Keeping her occupied with activities wasn't just a way to pass the time — it became something far more meaningful, more than just a coping mechanism.

Still, the night before every hospital visit filled us with anxiety. The uncertainty of what the doctors might say, what decisions might be made about Donna's future, was an ever-present, mind-bending worry. Yet, as the weeks went by, something incredible happened — the hospital visits became less frequent. Each time we returned, the Consultant was more astonished by Donna's improving blood profile. He openly admitted to being *'baffled.'*

One year later, Donna's progress defied all expectations. Her blood counts were now completely normal, and, to the Consultant's disbelief, she remained in remission.

'That'll do for me, and long may it continue,' was my silent thought. I didn't need explanations — as long as Donna was well, that was all that mattered.

Naturally, disciplining a child is an essential parental responsibility. But how do you enforce discipline when that child is expected to die? It felt like an impossible task.

Children quickly learn to take advantage of situations when there are no consequences for their actions, and Donna was no exception. Most of the time, discipline was non-existent if she misbehaved. But now, it was time to correct that mistake. Even seriously ill children need to understand right from wrong — though, after letting things slide for so long, making that transition was far from easy.

Between our many trips to Blackpool, Donna was granted a special experience by the charity *'Dreams Come True.'* However, it wasn't just a trip to London — Donna had adored Jason Donovan for years, and at that moment, he was starring in Joseph and the Technicolor Dreamcoat. Not only did she get to see the show, but she also had the incredible opportunity to meet Jason afterward.

The weeks of countless trips to Blackpool turned into months, and Donna grew physically stronger than she had ever been. Though still vulnerable to infections and with a fragile immune system due to chemotherapy, her overall recovery continued to defy expectations.

Even the oncologist and haematologist admitted they were utterly baffled. They had no medical explanation for Donna's inexplicable turnaround.

It was around this time that Donna expressed a new desire — she wanted to go to school. Her friends had started some weeks earlier, but we had been advised against sending her, as she remained immunocompromised. Yet, seeing her eagerness, we knew we had a difficult decision ahead.

But how could we possibly deny her this wish?

After discussing it with the hospital, the doctors agreed that sending Donna to school could be beneficial — helping her regain a sense of normality. And so, we began making preparations for her first day.

On that morning, Donna was fully kitted out in her new school uniform, looking every bit the excited student. She was a picture of determination, though her hair was only just beginning to grow back. My greatest concern wasn't her enthusiasm — it was the potential ridicule she might face, whether for her short hair or her academic struggles.

Children can be cruel, especially to those who are different. The thought of Donna being teased filled me with anxiety, a sickening unease settling deep in my stomach as I led her towards the school. That walk was, without a doubt, one of the most poignant journeys of my life. But for Donna, it was an adventure — an exciting new chapter.

As we arrived at the playground, the school whistle blew, signalling the start of the day. A lump formed in my throat, refusing to go away. I forced a brave smile as Donna turned to me, waved, and disappeared through the doors for the first time.

At least twice that day, I deliberately walked past the school, hoping for a glimpse of my little girl, desperate to reassure myself that she was okay.

My fears, however, proved to be unfounded. Donna came home that afternoon absolutely euphoric, brimming with stories about her newfound friends and the lessons she had enjoyed. The teachers had thoughtfully spoken with her classmates beforehand, explaining — at an age-appropriate level — that Donna had been very ill and needed their support.

For the first year, most of the children embraced this, offering her kindness and encouragement. But, as always, there were a few exceptions.

At first, school was a positive experience for Donna. But as time went on, it became clear that she was struggling — not just with the work, but also with some of the children who, at times, teased and taunted her.

Children can be cruel, and to some extent, that is understandable. But what disgusted me was that one of Donna's teachers was actively highlighting her differences, making her feel even more isolated. She would make Donna sit at the front of the class, on the floor, facing the blackboard — singling her out in a way that was both humiliating and unfair.

Donna was deeply upset by this, but it had been going on for some time before I even found out. One of her classmates mentioned it to me while playing with Donna, and I was absolutely furious. There was no way I was going to let this go.

I immediately demanded a meeting with both the head teacher and this particular teacher. How could someone who called themselves an educator behave this way? How could they justify such treatment? Furthermore, I insisted that it stop immediately. The head teacher, though weak and hesitant, assured me that steps would be taken to put an end to it. As Donna's parents, it was our duty to act — we would have been failing her had we not intervened.

Children naturally follow the example set by adults, and this teacher's actions had essentially given some of the student's permission to tease and ridicule Donna. The bullying — because that's exactly what it was — wasn't going to disappear on its own.

Aside from the emotional distress, we also began to notice that Donna's speech, reading, and writing skills seemed to be lagging behind those of children her age. This raised even more concerns. We feared that her education was suffering, and we knew it needed further investigation.

The head teacher wanted Donna to continue as she was, but I strongly disagreed. This wasn't in her best interest. So, I took matters into my own hands and contacted the educational psychology department for an official assessment. It was the right move.

The results confirmed that Donna had a mild cognitive deficit and specific educational needs — a learning disability. This wasn't entirely surprising. Learning disabilities are known to occur in children who have epilepsy, in those who have battled cancer in early childhood, and even in some cases of adoption or fostering.

Regardless of the cause, it became clear that Donna's learning deficit could not be effectively addressed in mainstream education. As a result, she was placed in Barbara Priestman School, in Sunderland, a specialized school for children with both physical and cognitive challenges. Unlike her previous experience, this school fostered a strong sense of community, with a genuine rapport between students and teachers.

On the medical front, in 1990, Donna attended her routine six-month follow-up appointment. But this time, she wasn't seen by just one Consultant — she was examined by three. As always, she greeted them with her infectious smile, but not one of them could provide an explanation for her incredible recovery. And then, something remarkable happened: Donna was officially discharged from further follow-ups and declared cured.

Some things in life don't need an explanation. For me, this was one of those times.

Donna's time at Barbara Priestman School was largely happy. The school placed a strong emphasis on personal development, believing that every child had a unique talent or skill waiting to be nurtured. When asked about her interests, Donna expressed a keen desire to improve her swimming — a choice that would prove to be incredibly significant in the years to come.

However, the aftereffects of her treatment had left their mark. Following intensive chemotherapy, Donna developed epilepsy — a condition that, according to every expert we consulted, would be extremely difficult to control with conventional antiepileptic medication.

For nearly three years, Donna suffered hundreds of mini-seizures daily. One medication after another failed to make a difference. Yet, despite these challenges, she remained determined to pursue swimming — an activity not typically associated with epilepsy.

Contrary to common misconceptions, it is safe for individuals with epilepsy to swim, provided they have a designated spotter — someone on the poolside trained to respond in case of an emergency. This safeguard allowed Donna to follow her passion while ensuring her safety.

Little did we know, this decision would soon open doors we never imagined possible.

It soon became clear that Donna was more than just an average swimmer. Her school did everything possible to nurture and encourage her talent.

Let me say a very special thank you to Steve Russell, Donna's swimming coach. Steve invested so much time and fervour to Donna's swimming that she would never have achieved what she did, without his support and dedication.

Wanting to further develop her technique, I enrolled her in a local swimming club, where she worked exceptionally hard, dedicating herself to improvement. Her efforts paid off — not only did she become an adept swimmer, but the sport also gave her a newfound sense of confidence.

Despite her cognitive deficits, Donna excelled in the water. She comfortably earned dozens of certificates and, when it came to swimming, she believed in herself completely. She could swim for miles without hesitation, finding a sense of freedom and strength in the water that she rarely experienced elsewhere.

Every year, Donna's school participated in a regional swimming competition at Darlington's Dolphin Centre. The event featured various races, and for those who performed well, it could open doors to national competitions — even potential selection for the England swim team.

That year, Donna was entered into no fewer than six races. Her nerves were obvious, but I reassured her: This isn't about your disability — this is about your ability. I reminded her that everyone has something they're good at. It's just a matter of discovering it and honing it. If you believe you can do it, you can do it!

As the first race approached, Donna's anxiety became more evident. She was physically shaking, doubt creeping into her mind. I watched, my own stomach in knots, as she stepped onto the starting block.

I marched up and down the poolside nervous and concerned, my stomach churning, and I hoped she would remember everything about reacting to the gun and getting a good start as she had been taught.

'*Take your marks.*'

Then — BANG!

Donna launched off the block like a bullet, slicing through the water with precision, her movements fluid and powerful. She took an early lead, gliding effortlessly.

But then, halfway through the first length, something went wrong.

Suddenly, Donna slipped beneath the water, floundering. Time seemed to slow. What felt like minutes was, in reality, only seconds — but those seconds felt like an eternity

I scanned the pool in horror, expecting the lifeguards to react. But they didn't.

Despite being informed beforehand that Donna had epilepsy, they hesitated. She was clearly in the midst of a seizure, yet no one moved.

I didn't think — I just ran.

Without a second thought, I sprinted along the poolside and dove in, fully clothed. At the same moment, Steve, Donna's swimming instructor, realized what was happening. He, too, dove into the water, both of us racing to reach her.

Donna was quickly pulled to the side and made a full recovery from the incident. I won't go into detail about what I said to the lifeguards — but I'm sure you can imagine.

But the story didn't end there.

What happened next was nothing short of remarkable. Despite the seizure, Donna insisted on continuing with her remaining five races. And even more incredibly, she went on to win three silver medals and two golds that day.

What an achievement!

Yet, this was only the beginning of her swimming journey.

On the bus ride home, the other students cheered for Donna, congratulating her on her success. At the same time, they had a good laugh at Mr. Russell and me for our unexpected dip in the pool — a moment that became the stuff of school legend.

Donna had now tasted competitive success, and for the first time in her life, she realized she had a talent — something she truly excelled at. And once she knew what she was capable of, she was determined to push herself even further.

With renewed excitement, she dedicated herself to training harder and longer. She used her allowance to buy the best equipment she could find, giving herself every possible advantage. Despite her educational deficits, she became highly knowledgeable about qualifying times for different competitions and events, studying them with meticulous focus.

Year after year, Donna competed at the Darlington swimming gala, bringing home dozens of medals. On one occasion, she even had the chance to meet Tony Blair, who attended the event to support the competitors. When he later became Prime Minister, she loved to tell the story of how she had met him long before he took office.

Her achievements didn't go unnoticed. Donna became a regular feature in the local press, earning widespread recognition and numerous awards for her swimming prowess.

Of course, when competing against able-bodied club swimmers, she didn't always place as highly. But rather than feeling discouraged, she used these experiences as motivation, always striving to improve.

Then, in 1995, a life-changing opportunity arrived.

Donna was invited to Rugby to try out for the England swimming team under the English Sports Association for People with Learning Disabilities. This was a dream come true — an opportunity to receive top-class coaching from nationally recognized instructors and, perhaps, the chance to represent her country.

After her trial, the head coach invited Donna to attend the next training session. From that point on, she became a regular at the England training camp. Though it would take some time before she officially joined the team for a major event, she was determined to prove herself.

The camaraderie within the team was incredible. The athletes were supportive of one another, and every three months, they would come together for training — something Donna eagerly looked forward to.

A few years later, a moment of immense pride arrived — Donna was selected to represent England at the **Danish Open Swimming Championships** in Copenhagen. I had the privilege of accompanying her, witnessing first-hand the culmination of years of dedication and perseverance.

She returned home with just one medal, but far more importantly, she brought back invaluable experience. I had always told Donna that medals were secondary; what truly mattered was giving her absolute best. And as long as she did that, she had nothing to regret.

Donna's skills continued to develop beyond recognition, and she became eager to push herself even further. She wanted to train alongside able-bodied swimmers who could challenge her in new ways. After researching our options, I managed to get her into **Chester-le-Street Swimming Club** — a move that would prove to be an excellent decision.

Though international competitions for athletes with learning disabilities were limited, Donna remained a dedicated member of the English Sports Association for People with Learning Disabilities and continued to represent England for many years. We travelled across the country, competing in countless events, collecting trophies and medals, and making lifelong friends along the way.

That same year, another extraordinary opportunity arose — this time, off the swimming pool deck and onto the football field. In September 1998, Newcastle United faced Manchester United at St. James' Park. I was among the capacity crowd that witnessed the Magpies dominate the Red Devils from start to finish, securing a stunning 5-0 victory.

After the match, the legendary Alan Shearer was awarded the Premier League Player of the Month award. But what made this moment even more special was his decision to dedicate the award to the English Sports Association for People with Learning Disabilities.

Even more incredibly, Donna was chosen to accept the award on behalf of the association. Naturally, I was right there beside her, sharing in yet another unforgettable moment in her journey.

In late 1996, Donna received a nomination for the prestigious McDonald's Child of Achievement Award, a testament to her remarkable swimming accomplishments following her recovery from leukaemia. She travelled to London for a gala event, where she met stars from the world of sports and media. The highlight of the evening came when she was presented with her award by the Right Honourable John Major, the Prime Minister at the time.

It was a moment that felt like a world away from the heartbreak of eleven years earlier when her precious life had seemed to hang by a thread. But Donna's journey was far from over. In 1998, something incredible happened — she caught the attention of the head coach of the Great Britain Paralympic team.

Unbeknownst to her, he had been tracking her performance in specific swimming events, and against all odds, she had worked her way into contention for a coveted spot on the national team set to compete in the World Swimming Championships in Christchurch, New Zealand. The final place came down to Donna and another young athlete. After an agonizing wait, the news she had been dreaming of finally arrived — she had secured her place on the team.

The day her Great Britain tracksuit arrived in the post, I watched with immense pride as she tried it on, standing tall in the red, white, and blue. Over the following months, she poured every ounce of her determination into training, pushing herself harder than ever. Her journey even caught the attention of the local television station, which featured her preparations for the championship.

Then, the long-awaited day arrived. Donna was set to meet the rest of the Great Britain team at Heathrow Airport, ready to embark on the adventure of a lifetime. That morning, as we boarded the train to London, something special happened. At Durham station, a businessman approached her with a warm smile.

'*I saw you on TV the other night,*' he said. '*Wishing you all the best — you'll do great.*'

Donna simply smiled, while I stood beside her, feeling ten feet tall with pride.

Though I couldn't travel to New Zealand with her, I followed her every move from afar, receiving updates over the phone after each race. When she swam the heats of the 50-meter breaststroke — her signature event — she gave it everything she had. Against the best in the world, she secured her place in the final.

It was more than just a competition. It was the realization of a dream, the culmination of years of resilience, and proof that the little girl who once fought for her life had become a champion in every sense of the word.

The following day, Donna stood on the brink of the biggest race of her life — the final. Eight swimmers would take their marks, and she was up against the fastest in the world. To stand a chance, she didn't just need a personal best — she needed to perform beyond anything she had ever done before. The odds were stacked against her; she had the slowest qualifying time. But making it to the final was already an incredible achievement.

And then, she did the extraordinary.

Donna swam her heart out, clocking a personal best and finishing sixth overall — a result beyond anything we had dared to dream. But her journey in New Zealand wasn't over yet. A few days later, she was selected to swim in both the 4 x100-meter and 4 x 50-meter freestyle relay teams. These races were fiercely competitive, each stroke a battle against the best in the world. And yet, the Great Britain girls' team rose to the challenge, securing second place in both events.

Donna was coming home from the 1998 World Swimming Championships with two silver medals.

I was the proudest father in the world. I told anyone who would listen about Donna's achievements — I couldn't help myself. The moment she returned home, I wanted her to know just how much she was celebrated, so I organized a surprise party, bringing together friends and family to honour her incredible success.

Donna was at the peak of her swimming career, more passionate and driven than ever before. A few months later, at a national competition in Reading, she entered several races, determined to keep pushing her limits. But the true highlight of the event came when she reunited with her Great Britain relay team. This time, they didn't just win.

They shattered a world record.

As triumphant as these moments were, there was a shadow that lingered in my heart — a regret that I struggle to put into words.

Donna's younger sister had quietly suffered in the background. Through the years of Donna's illness, the endless hospital visits, and the constant fear of relapse, my focus had been consumed by worry and survival. Even in recovery, Donna had unique challenges, requiring support for her cognitive deficits. I now realize that in trying to protect and care for one child, I unintentionally neglected the other.

There were times when she didn't get the parenting she deserved, moments that were lost forever. And no matter how much I wish I could turn back time, I cannot.

That is my greatest regret, a weight I will always carry.

I hope one day, that she will realize the complexity of that predicament, and understand that she was always, like Donna, loved unreservedly.

Chapter 11
My Belated Education

During the time that Donna had commenced her swimming career, life was, at last, returning to normal, and it was now that I had an important decision to make. A decision that would affect the rest of my life. Having accepted redundancy from my previous employment, it was now time to return to work. The big question was what would I do?

The answer was never in any doubt — nursing! I had developed a great respect and admiration for those who had nursed, encouraged and cajoled me through the real prospect of an early and premature death. I admired and respected the nurses who had more than just nursed Donna through a life-limiting disease; they had psychologically supported the whole family.

Lacking the necessary qualifications to pursue a nursing career, I made the decision to return to full-time education for a year to gain the credentials required for this new path in life. After being away from formal education for so long — and having once dismissed the system as unimportant — reintegrating proved challenging. I had to work exceptionally hard to keep up with my studies. Yet, paradoxically, I found the experience enjoyable.

During that academic year, I completed five GCSEs and one A-level. Though I could have spread this over two years, my eagerness to begin my nursing career drove me to complete it in just one. Despite achieving the necessary grades, gaining entry into a nursing program turned out to be more difficult than I had anticipated.

I interviewed with three nursing schools — Newcastle, Sunderland, and Gateshead. When asked about my motivation for pursuing nursing, I was completely honest about my history as a cancer survivor and my aspirations within the Health Service. Unfortunately, even at this stage, I encountered lingering prejudice and misconceptions about cancer survivorship within the very system meant to provide care and understanding.

Both Newcastle and Sunderland were impressed with my foresight and determination to make nursing a successful career and offered me a place there and then. Sadly Gateshead, which was my first choice of venue to train, felt that because of my background, they could not offer me a student place.

Taking a place at Gateshead would have allowed me to gain employment in my home town hospital, South Shields; the hospital which fourteen years earlier had made my cancer diagnosis.

Although disappointed, the belligerence of these nursing leaders left me confused, but I was content to ignore their obstinacy and accept a training place at Newcastle. My immediate aim was to qualify, and then work on ward 38 at Newcastle General, where I had received much of my treatment. However, one day, I wanted to return to my native South Shields to work in my hometown hospital and give something back to the local community, specifically in cancer care.

In May 1989, I commenced nurse training with pride and expectation. The training was hard work but very enjoyable, and I was fortunate to train with a great group of student nurses. They were almost all females and I had the unenviable distinction of being the oldest student in the group and, jokingly, they never let me forget that.

After an initial six weeks in the classroom, we were all allocated to a ward to spend ten weeks gaining knowledge and experience in the nursing profession. But, that was only the beginning as nurse training would take three years to complete. My first ward was a busy surgical unit, and I could not wait to start.

However, I would soon have the enthusiastic wind knocked out of my sails. The ward was a busy ward dealing mostly with abdominal surgery, much of which was for malignant disease. In the first few days, I looked after a little old chap, who appreciated a chat as much as the direct nursing care required for his condition.

Not everyone appreciated my friendly approach. One day, the ward sister summoned me to her office, where she wasted no time in setting me straight. She firmly stated that I was becoming too familiar with the patients and reminded me that my role was to learn — not to befriend them.

Her words took me by surprise. To me, nursing was rooted in communication and compassion, yet she seemed intent on maintaining an emotional distance between staff and patients. Wasn't connection a fundamental part of care? Though I strongly disagreed, I was just a student nurse and chose to remain silent. Wanting to be the best nurse I could, I accepted her reprimand, even though I knew deep down that she was wrong.

In many ways, her rigid approach only fuelled my determination to be a compassionate and dedicated nurse. Throughout my career, I encountered nurses of all kinds — some deeply caring and skilled, others lacking both warmth and respect, especially when it came to student nurses. I never forgot the way some senior staff spoke to and treated those still learning, often with a startling absence of kindness or encouragement.

I concluded that if they could treat student nurses with such contempt, then what was their actual patient care like? It was those early days that made me determined not to follow the paths of those with a negative and dictatorial approach to their care, they were not good role models. Admittedly, some nurses do the profession a great disservice, but the vast majority are enthusiastic and dedicated to the cause.

I placed numerous endeavours on my theoretical work too, as it was important to be able to underpin the practical skills with cognitive ability. My first piece of work was on Hodgkin Lymphoma and mostly came from my own established knowledge and was reflected in the lecturer's comments, '*An obvious understanding and empathy of this condition.*'

My pride endorsed the fact that this was the right career for me. And in those early days, it was a pleasure and a privilege to be influencing the health of people dependent upon nurses and doctors in the health service. Even for those individuals who were terminally ill, to be part of a team that could improve their symptoms and makes their dying days peaceful and pain-free was worth more than any salary I would receive.

In my second year of nurse training, I got the opportunity to spend a ten-week placement in ward 38. I did wonder how I would feel nursing patients in the very same environment where I was, myself, a patient fifteen years previous. However, my fear and apprehension were unfounded, and it proved to be a happy ward to work on.

All the staff knew of my previous illness and were, without exception, fully supportive of me and all the other student nurses allocated to the ward. One of the Auxiliary nurses, Pat, was an Auxiliary when I was a patient, and naturally, we would reminisce about the years gone by. Being a nurse was a massive and steep learning curve and having worked in a shipyard previously, this was at the complete opposite end of the spectrum.

Still, my mind was made up and my goal was to attain a job as a staff nurse on ward 38 once I qualified. That would prove to be my motivation throughout some of the more difficult times. During my time in ward 38, I once again met with the two Consultants who had previously treated my lymphoma.

Indeed, I would often accompany them on ward rounds. It was, undoubtedly, a weird and perhaps unprecedented relationship. For the previous fifteen years, these doctors, I had known only as a patient. Now, they are colleagues, discussing and advising me on the management of their cancer patients entrusted into my care.

There were even specific times when the sister of the ward would approach me, and ask if she could tell certain patients about my story. Naturally, I never declined this request if it were to be of benefit to other individuals. On those occasions, patients would typically ask about the differences in treatment and how as an individual I coped with the sentence of a cancer diagnosis.

Clearly, a diagnosis of cancer still brings with it an unprecedented fear, but even in this honoured situation, it would have been wrong of me to say, '*I know what you are going through,*' because quite frankly, I didn't. Everyone's cancer journey is unique, as is a patient's individual experience.

Working in the stressful environment of cancer care causes many pressures — pressures that need to be released, and nurses are certainly well renowned for going out and enjoying themselves, it's called a release mechanism. There were numerous times throughout my training and beyond that, I would be invited out.

Most often I felt that I had to decline these social occasions as my wife at the time would create merry hell and make all kinds of ridiculous accusations and insinuations, such was her jealousy. Therefore, instead of allowing these situations to arise, I would simply make any excuse not to attend. Even on the few occasions I went out with various teams from different wards, I felt obliged to take my wife along; at least it saved me from getting too much grief on my return home.

During nurse training, I was allocated to various wards that would give me the maximum amount of experience. I spent ten weeks in one of the paediatric wards, and that gave a whole new dimension to nursing. It was not just the children who needed care; the parents required psychological support, and that presented a different challenge to your nursing skills.

Naturally, during each placement, the student nurse would be allocated a mentor, someone to supervise and support the student and to assess the skills you were to achieve on that placement. During those ten weeks, a difficult but enjoyable and educative placement, I spent most of my time caring for a small boy aged two, and I got to know his parents very well.

His condition was uncontrollable epilepsy brought on by a condition that resulted in his skull being misshapen and which also affected his brain. The child had spent most of his life in hospital in a vain attempt to control his epilepsy, and this reminded me very much of Donna.

Some six weeks into my placement, the Neurologist was considering whether brain surgery would help improve his condition. The decision was a very difficult one, both for the surgeons, and his parents, such were the risks involved in the procedure.

It was at this time that I made what I now consider to be a bad decision; I decided to ask if I could be present if and when the boy went to the theatre. Having reviewed the situation, the Neurologist decided to take the youngster to theatre and operate on his brain. The parents, although understandably very anxious and concerned about the procedure, said that they felt a little better because I was going to be in the theatre with him.

During the procedure, things went well in the first couple of hours and went according to plan. Sadly, things quickly deteriorated as the child began to experience problems and, sadly, he subsequently died in the operating theatre. This was the most harrowing experience of my student days so far, and not what I was expecting.

How on earth could I now face the parents, as they had such confidence in me being in the theatre with their little boy?

The Consultant Neurologist knew that I had a good rapport with the parents and asked if I would accompany him to break the tragic news to them. I certainly did not feel as though I could refuse his request, but this was not something I had been trained for, and neither was I prepared for such a situation.

The parents were waiting immediately outside the theatre, and before we even spoke a word, they knew things had not gone to plan. How can you try to console parents in that situation? There are simply no correct things to say and this was no exception, you cannot make that dreadful situation any easier for a parent.

I struggled to maintain my composure; such was the extent of their unbearable distress. In fact, strangely, they still felt comforted by the fact that I'd been in the theatre with their little boy. Once back on the ward I was inconsolable, one of my colleagues on the same ward as me tried in vain to comfort me but to no avail.

Life indeed was so cruel. Where's the justification, the reasoning for the loss of an innocent life being needlessly wasted? To this day, I keep a photograph of the youngster at home. Life as a student nurse was extremely difficult, but also very enjoyable, throwing up many new and unexpected challenges.

Hand in hand with the difficult situations that I would face on the wards, there were also the exams and coursework that needed to be submitted by specific deadlines. At last, during my third year, I got the opportunity to return to ward 38 and this proved to be my future motivation.

I knew within the first few hours of working on ward 38 during my final year, that once qualified, there was no other discipline I wanted to work in other than Oncology. I instinctively knew the reward of caring for individuals with different cancers, and what's more, I wanted to continue to work on ward 38.

Not only that, but I felt that I had the passion and the empathy, but also the dedication to deliver what is undoubtedly a difficult and unpredictable job. Managing the care of cancer patients and all the physical and psychological problems they encounter. In addition, I contended that it would also allow me to give something back in return for all the care and dedication I had received during my illness.

I had two more ward placements ahead of me, but I knew that none would compare to the fulfilment of caring for cancer patients. Looking after those undergoing chemotherapy and radiotherapy — as well as supporting those in the terminal stages of their illness — had been the most rewarding experience of my training.

After completing my penultimate placement, only one remained before my final examinations — the last hurdle to becoming a staff nurse, provided I passed. This final placement was designed to consolidate my management experience, and I could be assigned to any ward.

Determined to return to Oncology, I devised a plan. If I approached the allocation officer, shared a little of my personal history, and expressed my deep desire to work in Oncology, perhaps she would be sympathetic. So, I did just that. To my delight, she was incredibly supportive — and as a result, my final placement was secured on Ward 38.

Subsequently, I had my last student placement on ward 38 and not only did this fulfil my needs, but the staff there were superb. Irrespective of my bias towards Oncology, they were a first-class group of nurses, and in hindsight an excellent team delivering a high standard of care. At the end of the ten weeks on ward 38, I prepared myself for the final weeks in class and then, the final examination.

I had never been confident in exam situations, but I wanted this qualification more than anything. As my fellow students buzzed about their final placements and their anxieties over the upcoming exams, I focused on what I could control. I had prepared thoroughly, and there was nothing more I could study — it was all up to me now.

Despite my nerves, I felt a quiet confidence. I had worked hard over the past three years, and my dedication would carry me through. Just days before the exams, I received exciting news: a junior staff nurse position would soon be opening on Ward 38. The timing was perfect. I eagerly awaited the job posting, knowing this could be my chance.

The finals went better than I could have hoped — even a question on cancer management appeared, playing right into my strengths. I walked out of the exam feeling optimistic. But, as always, doubt crept in. I replayed my answers, questioning whether I had included enough detail, second-guessing myself. Now, all I could do was wait — weeks of uncertainty, anxiety, and hope.

In the meantime, the Ward 38 position was officially advertised. Without hesitation, I called personnel for an application form, which arrived two days later. I completed it immediately, eager to secure the role — on the assumption I had passed the final exam of course.

Back in the classroom, we received training on interview techniques, while some of my classmates had already attended interviews — several had even secured positions. My opportunity was coming, and I was determined to be ready.

The day had finally arrived — the results of my exams were due. I was up at the crack of dawn, drinking cup after cup of coffee until I was buzzing with nervous energy. Then, at last, I spotted the postman, casually swinging the gate open, strolling up the path, completely unaware that he held my future in his hands. The moment he pushed the letters through the letterbox, I rifled through the pile until I found the one I was waiting for.

With trembling hands, I ripped it open and read the words: '*I am pleased to tell you…*' I had done it. I had passed. Relief and joy flooded through me. From being diagnosed with cancer seventeen years earlier to having my world turned upside down by Donna's illness — everything had led to this moment. I was now a fully qualified nurse, determined to carve out a future in cancer care.

Ten days later, another letter arrived, fuelling my determination even further — I had secured an interview for the Ward 38 position. The day of the interview, I was on edge, my excitement bordering on anxiety. As I sat outside the interview room, my heart pounded so loudly I was sure it was distracting the other candidates.

When my turn came, I stood up, only to feel my legs turn to jelly. Could I even walk through the door? The interview panel greeted me with warm smiles, doing their best to put me at ease. The questions began, and for a moment, my tongue felt thick and uncooperative, as if it were wrapped in cotton wool. But gradually, I found my rhythm and got my answers out.

Time stretched endlessly as I sat under their scrutiny, but eventually, they thanked me and promised to call later that day. The hours that followed were unbearable — I couldn't focus on anything. One minute blurred into the next until, at last, the phone rang. The voice on the other end was instantly recognizable — the Sister from Ward 38.

She began by telling me that I had performed very well in the interview. While I was pleased to hear it, all I could think was, just get to the point! Then came the words that made my heart stop: '*We would like to offer you the post on Ward 38.*'

For once in my life, I was utterly speechless. My mind went blank, and when I finally managed to respond, I mumbled something incoherent. It probably made no sense, but it didn't matter — I had the job.

That night, in celebration, a bottle of Jim Beam was nearly emptied. Finally, everything was falling into place. I could now look forward to my career as a staff nurse — not just anywhere, but on Ward 38, the very place where I had found strength, support, and purpose.

Cancer survivorship was not just a journey — it was a triumph, and a virtue.

Chapter 12
Climbing the Ladder

Nursing in Ward 38 was both rewarding and demanding — an experience that shaped me profoundly. The environment was intense, often stressful, yet I spent several years there, gaining invaluable knowledge that became the foundation of my cancer nursing career.

The team was exceptional — a diverse group of professionals who supported one another, understood the power of teamwork, and embraced humour as a coping tool. Beyond refining my clinical skills, I also recognized the importance of education in nursing.

In my first few months as a newly qualified staff nurse, I attended college one day a week to complete a teaching certificate. Teaching quickly became an integral part of my practice and remained central throughout my career. I firmly believe that nursing and education go hand in hand. No one holds a monopoly on knowledge — sharing experiences fosters collaboration, strengthens teams, and ultimately enhances patient care.

My dual perspective — as both a nurse and a cancer patient — has profoundly influenced my approach to care. Experiencing illness first-hand gave me invaluable insight into the vulnerabilities, fears, and needs of patients in a way that textbooks and training alone could never provide. It deepened my empathy, sharpened my ability to recognize unspoken concerns, and reinforced the importance of compassionate, patient-centred care. It also made me acutely aware of the significance of clear communication and reassurance, as I had once been in their position, searching for answers and comfort.

Perhaps most importantly, my experience as a father of a child with cancer further shaped my understanding of holistic care. It reinforced the reality that illness affects not only the individual but also their loved ones. I learned that true nursing extends beyond clinical expertise; it encompasses emotional support, advocacy, and the ability to walk alongside patients and their families during their most challenging moments.

This perspective also influenced my approach to mentorship. Just as I benefited from the knowledge of others, I believe it is my duty to pass on what I have learned. The wisdom I share with students and colleagues is not mine alone

— it is a collection of lessons gained from my experiences as a patient, a father, and a nurse. One of the most significant conversations I ever had with a student nurse was not shaped solely by my professional training, but by my lived experience. That conversation, and many others like it, underscored the importance of bridging the gap between clinical knowledge and human experience in nursing practice.

A student nurse who incidentally was very enthusiastic and determined to learn said to me during a busy early morning shift, '*Cancer patients appear happy and well-adjusted, they cope very well?*'

Now, this statement stuck in my mind and served as a good example of the stereotypical attitude of many individuals, students and qualified nurses alike. My response on this occasion was, '*Remember, we only see these patients when they are on the ward, we don't see them when they are at home.*'

I think this is a critical point; nurses can go off-duty at the end of a shift, forgetting all about cancer care until the next day. In contrast, cancer patients do not have the opportunity to go off-duty; they are permanently on duty, regardless of where they are or what time of the day it is. Often, the perception the cancer patient portrays is a brave face, coping with all that life throws at them and being able to cope and carry on with life normally. This, in my view, is a false perception.

I would perhaps argue that in the main, this is a false illusion, not because they deliberately want to deceive health care professionals. It is simply that we do not realize the difficulties the cancer patient faces when away from the safety and security of a dedicated health care environment. On another occasion, one of my patients, an elderly lady with terminal cancer, was talking about the times she enjoyed during her childhood.

She began telling me that one of her fondest childhood memories was performing cartwheels for her disabled brother. As she recounted this with a smile, I had a sudden inspiration — I would demonstrate my own cartwheeling skills right there in the hospital ward. Without hesitation, I launched into a series of cartwheels along the corridor, much to her delight.

Unfortunately, just as I was mid-cartwheel, the departmental manager entered the ward. Her face hardened with disapproval as she ordered me to stop immediately and report to her office. Flushed with embarrassment, I followed her, my heart sinking. In her office, she delivered a stern reprimand, calling my behaviour foolish and unprofessional. I tried to explain — there had been no harm done, no obstacles in my way, and most importantly, I had brought joy to a dying woman. But my reasoning fell on deaf ears. I was firmly instructed never to engage in such '*idiotic*' behaviour again.

Three days later, the lady for whom I had performed my acrobatics passed away. However, the patient in the opposite bed later told me that she had spoken fondly to her family about my impromptu performance, cherishing that moment of light-heartedness in her final days. Despite the reprimand, I knew in my heart that I had done something meaningful.

Twelve months later, I completed my teaching certificate and was eager to pursue further education — something that would have a direct impact on patient care. After much consideration, I applied for a scholarship to Birmingham University to study clinical hypnotherapy. I was drawn to hypnotherapy not only for its potential in clinical practice but also for the profound impact it could have on my nursing career as a whole.

At the time, hypnotherapy was an underappreciated therapeutic tool, yet it held immense potential to enhance the well-being of cancer patients, alleviating both the debilitating side effects of treatment and the symptoms of the disease itself. Upon completing my certificate in Clinical Hypnotherapy, I became one of only a handful of nurses practicing this therapy within the UK's health service — an achievement I held with immense pride.

Over the years, I witnessed first-hand the transformative power of hypnotherapy. Countless patients found relief through this complementary therapy, reinforcing my belief in its value. Even as early as 1994, research suggested that more than 70% of cancer patients had considered using complementary therapies at some point in their journey. While these treatments were never meant to replace conventional medicine, they played a vital role in holistic patient care.

Every day, cancer patients present healthcare professionals with new challenges. Yet, despite the difficulties, it remains a privilege to do this work.

While practicing at Newcastle, I continued to see Dr. Bozzino and Dr. Atkinson annually for my own check-ups, but our interactions extended beyond that — I now saw them regularly in a professional capacity.

My journey, from performing cartwheels in a hospital ward to pioneering clinical hypnotherapy in nursing, has been one of unexpected turns and profound fulfilment. It has taught me that sometimes, the smallest moments — whether a simple acrobatic display or the calming voice of a hypnotherapist — can leave the deepest impact on those in need.

At my next appointment, Dr. Bozzino decided to discharge me from his follow-up clinics, reassuring me that if I had any concerns, I should contact him immediately. However, he did not expect that I would need to.

Eighteen months later, much to my concern, I found myself reaching out to him once again. Without warning, I began experiencing searing, excruciating pains in my head. The sensation was as if a red-hot needle were being driven into my skull — sudden, fleeting, yet utterly agonizing. The unpredictability of these attacks, striking at any hour of the day or night, left me shaken.

Fearing the worst, I contacted Dr. Bozzino, just as he had advised. Though he wasn't certain of the cause, he couldn't rule out the possibility of a malignant relapse. Without hesitation, he arranged an emergency brain CT scan, insisting it be done as soon as possible.

Yet even a week's wait felt like an eternity. Every sleepless night was consumed by anxiety, my mind racing through terrifying possibilities. What if my cancer had returned? I kept my fears to myself, telling no one — not family, not friends, not colleagues. I didn't want to burden them, but in doing so, I denied myself the comfort of their support.

How would I cope with a relapse? I had believed I was cured, that I had put this chapter behind me. The thought of facing it all again — physically, emotionally, psychologically — was overwhelming. Cancer survivorship, I was beginning to understand, was far from straightforward.

As the day of the scan drew closer, my dread deepened. I convinced myself that this was, indeed, a recurrence. And then, at last, the results came.

No evidence of malignancy.

Relief washed over me, yet the question remained — what was causing these unbearable headaches? Since this was beyond Dr. Bozzino's expertise, he referred me to a neurologist.

Later that month, I met with a specialist who finally provided an answer. I was suffering from a type of migraine known as 'ice pick' headaches, triggered by stress and anxiety. And stress, I certainly had plenty of. Though the pain was real, at least it was not something more sinister. Perhaps, now that I had an explanation, these attacks would settle.

Around this time, I had just completed an advanced Oncology course — an important milestone for nurses caring for cancer patients. Shortly after, I was offered a temporary position as a higher-grade staff nurse on Ward 37, working primarily with female cancer patients.

Stepping into this role, I carried not only my professional knowledge but also a deeply personal understanding of fear, uncertainty, and survival. I had walked that path myself. Now, I had the opportunity to use my experience to guide others through their own journeys.

This position was set for six months, meant to prepare me for a permanent higher-grade role when one became available on Ward 38.

After eighteen months in Oncology, I couldn't have been any happier, doing meaningful, fulfilling work. I felt ready to take on more responsibility. My colleagues agreed and encouraged me to apply for the next available post. Yet, despite my readiness, it would take another eight months and three interviews before I finally secured a permanent position.

It never ceases to amaze me how fate works.

One morning, during a particularly busy shift on Ward 38, I stepped out of the lift and was met by the frail figure of a young man. His face was pale, his expression etched with fear. I had seen that same look before — in the mirror, during my own battle.

Sweat glistened on his forehead as he introduced himself in a trembling voice — Simon (name changed). The ward was overwhelmed that Friday morning, and I didn't have time to attend to him immediately. Instead, I led him, his brother, and his pregnant girlfriend into the day room, promising to return as soon as I could.

Barely five minutes later, I was pulled away from the drug trolley by Simon's brother. His voice was laced with urgency. Simon, gripped by fear, had made a decision — he was going to leave. He wanted to abandon chemotherapy and return home.

Everything else faded in that moment. I knew how crucial it was for Simon to start treatment for his mediastinal Teratoma. Without hesitation, I handed off my duties to a colleague and turned my full attention to him.

I led Simon, his brother, and his girlfriend into the quiet room — the very same room I had once occupied with Syd, many years earlier.

I understood this moment all too well. But this time, I wasn't the patient. This time, I was the one offering strength.

I couldn't simply walk into that room and blurt out that I had also had cancer and knew what Simon was going through. First, I had no idea what was truly going through his mind. And second, this moment wasn't about me — I needed to let Simon lead.

In the privacy of the quiet room, Simon confided in me. He had heard so much about chemotherapy, and he was convinced he couldn't endure the side effects. His voice wavered as he spoke, his eyes filled with unshed tears. I could feel the emotion in the room, and I won't deny that it affected me, too.

Simon acknowledged that his fears were largely shaped by the way chemotherapy is portrayed in the media — the horror stories that paint a picture of relentless suffering. Stories that often do more harm than good, leading patients to expect the worst, even when those side effects may never come. I took the time to explain what he might experience, emphasizing that these were only possibilities, not certainties. Slowly, I could sense a shift in him — our conversation was building a foundation of trust.

Despite my limited experience as a staff nurse, I made a monumental decision — one that could have gone either way. I chose to share a part of my own story. I told Simon about my own fears and anxieties when I had faced treatment, about the uncertainty that had once consumed me.

What happened next was something I could never have predicted.

We discovered that we had far more in common than just a cancer diagnosis. We were both from South Shields. We both had a deep love for rock music and Newcastle United Football Club. And we both enjoyed horse racing — the sport of kings — though neither of us had much luck with it.

For Simon, chemotherapy was the most terrifying ordeal of his 32-year existence. I knew that fear intimately. I had lived it myself, eighteen-years earlier. And somehow, fate had brought me full circle — from sitting in that very room as a frightened young man, uncertain of my future, to now sitting there with Simon, offering reassurance and understanding in his own battle.

From that moment on, Simon sought my thoughts and experiences before every procedure. The medical and nursing staff recognized the unique bond we had formed and fully supported it. It's important to say that I don't share my personal story with every patient — I know that it's not always the right approach. But with Simon, I instinctively knew it was. And I was right.

Simon's first admission was fraught with complications. Recurrent infections prolonged his hospital stays, making his journey far more difficult. Ironically, despite his initial fears, he suffered very few side effects from the chemotherapy itself. But his battle was relentless. Setback followed setback, and despite months of fighting, his disease remained uncontrolled.

A bone marrow investigation confirmed our worst fears — extensive infiltration. The cancer was progressing.

The day came when Simon and his girlfriend sat down with the consultant and Macmillan nurse. They were told, face to face, that he would not recover.

His girlfriend was devastated — her eternal optimism, shattered in an instant. But Simon? He simply nodded. He said he had always known this would happen. And in a strange way, he seemed relieved.

A few weeks later, Simon passed away at home, surrounded by the people who loved him.

It was undeniably heart-breaking. And yet, I have no hesitation in including this experience in my chronicle. Because despite the sorrow, there was something deeply meaningful about the connection we had formed. A reminder of why I do what I do. A testament to the power of understanding, empathy, and human connection.

Yes, despite modern-day advances in cancer care, Simon did die. But, on so many occasions, he imparted to me how important our relationship was to him. Furthermore, at a time when, as a staff nurse, I was still consolidating my nurse training, this positive incident has had a great impact on my clinical practice and I feel it has moulded my practice today.

A few weeks after Simon's death, I received the most fantastic letter from the family thanking me for my input in Simon's management. What greater thanks could there be? There is, however, something from this situation that I call survivor guilt — despite my support and care for Simon and his loved ones, the fact that he died, and I was still alive, made me feel strangely guilty, a bizarre emotion that I would experience many times over the years to follow.

So, why do nurses working in the discipline of cancer services do what they do? Simply, because they are compassionate, and committed because they want to make a difference. They accept that it is a privilege to be involved with these patients, yet by the very nature of the disease, the fact is many patients will lose their battle, making this a stressful and difficult job; leading nurses to confront their own mortality.

In my view, just because someone has a piece of paper, representing a diploma, or a degree, does not mean that they are any better at doing the job than the person who does not have that qualification. I sometimes think that far too much emphasis these days is given to those pieces of parchment; it could also be argued that it attracts the wrong kind of person into the profession, a person who might see nursing as an access route to a degree.

Of course, education is vital so that we can continue to grow, and mature cognitively. But nurses caring for cancer patients need empathy, commitment, and above all, good communication skills to make a difference for the simple reason that if we fail then so do our cancer patients. We would also fail the patient's family, and that negative experience can leave a permanent psychological scar that is difficult to overcome and detracts from their quality of life. This makes employing the right people in cancer services fundamental.

Less than five years after qualifying, I felt it was time to broaden my horizons. My ultimate goal had always been to work at South Tyneside, the very place where my original diagnosis had been made. However, opportunities for progression beyond Ward 38 were scarce, and I was ready to take the next step.

Despite my ambition, the thought of moving on gave me pause. Ward 38 had been more than just a workplace — it was where I had come full circle, from patient to staff nurse, surrounded by a team that felt like family. Leaving would not be easy. But I knew that to grow, I needed broader experience.

After much deliberation, I decided to apply for a Charge Nurse position in the chemotherapy day unit at Sunderland Royal Hospital. It was a role that would challenge me, expose me to new aspects of cancer care, and bring me closer to my long-term career aspirations.

Unbeknownst to me, a colleague from Ward 38, Lucy (name changed), had also applied for the same position. She had more experience and already held a degree — something I was still working toward. We were both shortlisted for interviews alongside candidates from other hospitals.

I remember feeling confident as I left the interview, believing I had presented myself well. We were told that the decision would be announced the following day.

The next morning, both Lucy and I were on duty when the phone rang. I answered. It was the personnel officer from Sunderland, asking to speak with Lucy. My heart sank — I knew what that meant. And sure enough, Lucy had been offered the job.

Thirty minutes later, the phone rang again. This time, it was for me. The personnel officer informed me that I had not been successful.

I congratulated Lucy without hesitation — she had earned it. But deep down, I couldn't ignore the sting of disappointment.

Still, I reminded myself that this was only my first attempt at securing a senior position outside of Newcastle General Hospital. There would be other opportunities. And when the right one came, I would be ready.

As someone who believes in fate, I accepted the situation. But just seven days later, Lucy made a surprising decision — she chose to take her career in a different direction and withdrew her acceptance of the senior position. I knew this meant the post would now be offered to someone else. But if it was offered to me, would I accept it? Could I take a role knowing I had been the second choice?

Then came the call. The position was mine if I wanted it.

I asked for the weekend to consider my decision, promising to call back on Monday. I wrestled with my thoughts, questioning whether I was making the right choice. But deep down, I knew this was an opportunity too significant to turn down. It was a crucial stepping stone toward my ultimate goal. And so, after much deliberation and soul-searching, I accepted the prestigious position.

Managing a department and leading a team was an entirely new challenge. Stepping into the chemotherapy day unit at Sunderland Royal Hospital, I was eager to introduce myself to the team I would be working with. It was a small, tight-knit group, all highly experienced in chemotherapy administration.

To my surprise, I already knew some of them. Paula, whom I had studied with when earning my teaching certificate five years earlier, and June, whom I had first met years before when she had lived nearby during Donna's illness. Donna had played with her daughter, Emma, back then. These familiar faces gave me a sense of reassurance as I stepped into my new role.

I embraced the challenge, not just as a test of my managerial skills but as a chance to make a real difference in patient care. During my three years in the post, I received overwhelmingly positive feedback — from patient satisfaction surveys, from senior management, from my colleagues. But most importantly, from the patients and their families. I knew I had achieved my goal.

One of the most unexpected yet invaluable aspects of this journey was my friendship with June. From the moment I took on the manager's role, we formed an instant connection. We understood each other, supported each other, and instinctively knew when the other needed to talk.

Our bond was so strong that it didn't take long for colleagues to speculate — suggesting, in the way only nurses can, that there was something romantic between us. But nothing could have been further from the truth. We were confidantes, not lovers. In June, I found a friend like no other, someone I could truly rely on.

And perhaps, in some ways, I needed that friendship more than I had realized.

I had confided in my sister Allyson twelve years earlier that my marriage wasn't working and that I was deeply unhappy. But for the sake of my children, leaving was never an option — not while they were young and in need of stability. They were innocent in all of this, and I wanted to shield them from the turmoil.

Yet, I never shared my unhappiness with my wife. To do so would have made life unbearable — not just for me, but for my daughters as well. I told myself that when Donna and her sister were old enough to understand, I would end the marriage. That they would see that sometimes, two people are simply incompatible and need to go their separate ways.

But in my naivety, I had hoped for something unrealistic. I had imagined that we could part on good terms, that we could remain friends for the sake of our children. I believed we could handle the separation with maturity and mutual respect.

I was wrong.

That hope was an impossible one. And I was naive to ever think otherwise.

The marriage had reached an irretrievable point. Arguments had become a daily occurrence, often over trivial matters. But it wasn't just the constant bickering — there was something far deeper, an unspoken truth that neither of us could ignore any longer. The hardest part was knowing that our children were caught in the middle of a no-win situation, innocent victims of a failing marriage.

Professionally, it was an incredibly rewarding and fulfilling time, yet personally, it was one of the most difficult periods of my life. I did my best to keep the turmoil from my colleagues and, most importantly, from my children. But they weren't blind to the tension — Donna, now eighteen, had been aware of the fractures in our home for some time. As I faced the reality of my marriage's collapse, I had to seriously consider my future and the path I wanted to take.

Work became my sanctuary, a welcome distraction from the chaos at home. And during this time, June's friendship proved invaluable. Despite the cruel rumours that circulated, there was no romantic relationship between us — at least, not then. But something was drawing us together, something beyond explanation. Perhaps fate was, once again, weaving its own plans.

The divorce proceedings were hostile and emotionally exhausting. The children struggled with the situation, reluctant to take sides — at least in the beginning. Beyond this, I prefer not to dwell on the bitterness of that chapter. What matters is that I was fortunate to have the unwavering support of friends and family, who helped me navigate one of the most challenging transitions of my life.

Not long after, I realized that I needed a change — not just in my personal life, but in my career as well. I had managed the chemotherapy unit for three years, and I began searching for a new opportunity, something that would challenge me and provide a fresh sense of purpose.

That opportunity soon arrived in the form of a Chemotherapy Nurse Specialist role for a private company in the community. It seemed like the answer I had been looking for. I went through the interview process, was offered the position, and accepted it, hopeful that this would be the next step in my professional journey.

But within months, I realized I had made a mistake.

From the beginning, it became clear that the role was not what I had anticipated, or told it was. As the most experienced practitioner, I was burdened with a disproportionate amount of responsibility, particularly in training and overseeing newer nurses who lacked the necessary expertise. I had been misled about the level of support available, and to make matters worse, I found some of their practices deeply concerning — at times, bordering on unsafe.

Despite my misgivings, I remained in the role for a few years, knowing that even difficult experiences could provide valuable lessons. And then, fate intervened once more.

Karen joined the team.

I had worked with Karen years earlier in Newcastle, and I knew immediately that she was a tremendous asset. Highly skilled, knowledgeable, and meticulous in her practice, she was one of the best nurses I had ever worked with. Her arrival transformed my experience in the role, restoring a sense of professionalism and support that had been missing.

And in the end, despite my initial reservations, this job — this unexpected detour — would lead me directly to my ultimate dream. For that, I would once again be grateful for the unpredictable hand of fate.

At that time, June remained my closest friend. Beyond our shared experiences in nursing, we were bound by the parallel struggles of our respective marriage breakups. Yet, our connection ran even deeper. She was there when I needed a shoulder to lean on, always offering rational and pragmatic advice despite her own worries and troubles.

I can't say when, and I can't say how, but somewhere along the way, our relationship shifted. What had been a deep friendship gradually evolved into something more — something neither of us had planned, but both of us embraced. It was, and remains, one of the best things to ever happen to me.

Love is one of the most powerful forces known to man, and yet it often arrives unannounced, without fanfare or planning. June and I were no exception. Without a word, without any deliberate decision, we simply fell in love. And from that moment, our relationship only grew stronger. We complemented each other perfectly; she knew my thoughts, and I knew hers. After everything, I had finally found my true soulmate.

Following the breakup of my marriage, I moved in with my Mam. I had a fantastic relationship with both of my parents, and in many ways, it was a comfort to be back home. But after almost ten months, I felt the pull to find a place of my own again.

Once again, fate stepped in.

I came across a seven-bedroom house listed at an unbelievably reasonable price. I didn't need that many rooms, but the price was too tempting to ignore. The owner had scheduled an open viewing, so I went along — with June by my side, of course.

The house was enormous, and while the price was good, it was clear it needed substantial work. More importantly, it didn't feel right — it lacked warmth, a sense of home. I dismissed it almost immediately.

As we were leaving, June happened to notice the house next door. It was also on the market — a similar Victorian property, but vacant. I took note of the estate agent's details and decided to inquire the next day.

I soon learned the house had been empty for nearly a year. Once again, fate had intervened.

I arranged a viewing and this time brought not only June but also her nine-year-old daughter, Sophie. The moment we stepped inside, I felt something different. Built in 1875, the house had real character. Despite needing considerable renovation, it had undeniable warmth — a comforting presence that made it feel like home.

I instinctively knew this was the one.

The following day, I made an offer. After months of back-and-forth, it was finally accepted. Every single room needed work, but I saw it not just as a home, but as an investment in the future.

Months later, we moved in — lock, stock, and barrel. The renovations would continue for years, but by September 1999, the same time Sir Bobby Robson took charge of my beloved Newcastle United, we had settled into our new home. It was still a work in progress, but it was ours. And for the first time in a long time, life felt exactly as it should be.

Our first Christmas together was unforgettable. It was the night I proposed to June. She hesitated for only a moment — just long enough to make my heart race — before saying yes. From that moment, our journey together truly began.

Not long after setting up our home, life threw us a surprise. First, Emma, June's eldest daughter, needed a place to stay. Without hesitation, we welcomed her in. Then, Donna, my own daughter, found herself in need of a refuge after a painful breakup. With nowhere else to turn, she naturally came to me. Without question, without a second thought, she too became part of our home.

There were challenges, of course. Sharing a home with adult children is never easy. But through it all, our love remained steadfast, our bond unshaken.

Time moved on, and so did Emma. She found love and started a new chapter with her boyfriend. Before long, she gifted us with something truly precious — our first granddaughter, Courtney — my princess.

Donna, too, built a life of her own, though much to my dismay, she settled in London. I would have loved to have her closer, but her happiness mattered more. Then, despite the pain she had endured in the past, she, too, blessed us with grandchildren — first Kieran, then Kara.

Courtney, as it turned out, would inherit more than just our love — she shared my passion for Hawkwind and Newcastle United, even becoming my season ticket companion. Moments like those made life even sweeter.

Then, in 2001, another dream took shape. A job posting appeared for a Haematology Clinical Nurse Specialist at South Tyneside Hospital — the very role I had longed for. There was no hesitation; I had to apply.

Still, doubt lingered. Submitting the application was one thing, but securing the job? That was another matter entirely. I knew competition would be fierce.

Weeks passed before the letter arrived — the one I had been waiting for. I had been shortlisted for an interview and would need to prepare a presentation. For the next two weeks, I was buried in my books, immersing myself in everything I needed to know.

Then came the day. The interview. The nervous wait. And finally, the phone call.

The job was mine.

The moment I hung up, I called June at work, barely able to contain my excitement. Next, I rang my manager, Karen, who had always known this was my dream. She was thrilled for me.

Stepping into that role felt like fate. I was returning to the very hospital where, twenty-six years earlier, my own diagnosis had been made. Life had come full circle. The legacy of survivorship had not just shaped me — it had led me home.

Since then, it has been both a pleasure and a privilege to provide haematology nursing care at South Tyneside District General Hospital. My role has encompassed many aspects of care — dedicated clinics, prescribing chemotherapy, difficult conversations, and, often, the heart-breaking task of breaking bad news to patients and their loved ones.

What makes this journey even more profound is the setting itself. The very rooms where I now stand as a nurse are the same ones where, years ago, I sat as a patient. The same room where I had received relentless rounds of chemotherapy. The room where doctors told me, more than once, that the treatment had failed. Where a junior doctor struggled, unsuccessfully, to retrieve a bone marrow sample from my fragile chest.

And now, in a twist of fate, I am the haematology nurse specialist — the one responsible for performing those very bone marrow investigations. Fate is a strange thing. You cannot predict it. You can tempt it. But I believe you cannot change it.

Working in haematology, caring for individuals battling the same cancers that both Donna and I fought, is a deeply moving experience. How does it make me feel? Humbled. Honoured. And, at times, haunted by survivor's guilt. I have stood beside so many who did not make it, and I have asked myself — why me? Why did I survive when so many others did not?

But more than anything, I am profoundly grateful. Every day, I am reminded of the responsibility I hold. My own experiences — both Donna's and mine — shape the care I provide. I can only hope that, through my work, I have made a difference in the lives of those I have been privileged to care for.

In 2004, the '**Agenda for Change**' legislation was introduced, requiring all nurses to justify their roles and complete detailed job descriptions, which would determine their pay grade. Eventually, I was awarded Band 8 — the highest banded cancer nurse at South Tyneside — and given the title of '*Head of Haematology Services.*' It was another moment where fate had lifted me to a new level of pride and purpose.

Of course, this role comes with its share of sorrow. I have seen far too many people lose their battle against cancer. If I had a pound for every patient I had cared for, I'd be a rich man. But in truth, I already am — wealthy not in money, but in the privilege of having been part of so many lives, each one leaving an imprint on my heart.

Forget about prizes and awards — and I have been fortunate to receive many in my career — but what greater accolade exists for a nurse than the heartfelt gratitude of the people they care for? At the heart of it all, nursing is about patient satisfaction, about making a difference in someone's most vulnerable moments.

It would be impossible to name all the incredible individuals I have had the privilege of caring for over the years. Each one has left a mark on me, their strength and resilience forever etched in my memory — testament to the human spirit in the face of adversity.

And truly, that is the greatest reward of all.

When someone we love dies, we are faced with two choices. We can close our eyes and dwell in sorrow, or we can open them, remembering them with love, cherishing the joy they brought into our lives. I say this with sincerity, never to diminish anyone's grief, but to offer a perspective that has helped me navigate loss.

Cancer nursing forces you to see life differently. It teaches you that time is precious, that dreams should never be postponed. Perhaps that's why, when I hit the age of forty-seven, I felt an undeniable urge — I wanted to learn to ride a motorbike.

Until that point, I had only been on the back of a motorbike twice in my life. I had never ridden one myself. And yet, the pull was strong. It wasn't just a whim; it was a dream I needed to fulfil.

June was apprehensive at first, but as always, she stood by me with unconditional support. So, I took the leap. I contacted a local training school, completed my basic training, passed the written exam, and eventually, after a second attempt, I earned my full riding license.

Now, I needed a bike. But not just any bike — it had to have character. I settled on a Daelim Daystar, a replica of the early Harley Indian. It was perfect for gaining experience, though I had my sights set on the real deal — a Harley.

There is nothing quite like the feeling of riding along the coast road, the wind against your face, the open road stretching endlessly ahead. It's freedom. It's escape. It's pure exhilaration.

For years, I rode a Suzuki Marauder 800cc, and though I never did get my Harley, I still hold on to that dream.

Meanwhile, life moved forward. Work remained fulfilling, and time with June was everything I could have hoped for. Through the years, we faced challenges, as all couples do, but never in our relationship. That foundation — our love — remained unshaken, solid as a rock. And I can say, with my hand on my heart, that in all our time together, we have never exchanged a cross word.

Some things in life are just meant to be.

On more than one occasion, June would playfully ask, '*When are you going to marry me?*'

My usual response? A flippant, '*At some point.*'

I had proposed back in 1999, so why did I always dodge the question? The truth was, I had a plan. It had always been my intention to organize everything in secret and then surprise her with a set wedding date.

I had already asked Terry to be my best man, checked with key family members to ensure they'd be available for our special day, and in 2003, I quietly booked the Town Hall for the following year — August 29, 2004, to be precise.

Rather than a traditional surprise proposal in a fancy restaurant with a ring — something I knew June wouldn't particularly appreciate — I wanted to do it in a way that felt more personal, more meaningful.

So when June suggested that we stay in for my birthday, I saw the perfect opportunity. With the wedding mostly arranged, I decided to propose again — this time, with a plan in place.

That night, the scene was set: candlelight, good food, and a nice bottle of wine to mark the occasion. I handed June a card, with a simple message, it was an invitation — to her own wedding. It included all the details, everything I had arranged.

For once in her life, June was speechless.

Of course, she said yes. It was a night we would cherish forever.

The arrangements were nearly complete — the ceremony, an afternoon reception at a charming Spanish tapas restaurant, and an evening celebration at The Sea Hotel. All that remained was one small detail: the music.

I told June she could choose the song to walk down the aisle to.

She hesitated. Then, in a moment that caught me completely off guard, she said she didn't want to walk down the aisle at all. Instead, she suggested that I do it.

Laughing, I joked, *'Fine, but if I'm walking down the aisle, it'll be to the sound of Hawkwind.'*

To my astonishment, June simply nodded and said, *'That's fine.'*

And the more I thought about it, the more it made perfect sense. Hawkwind had been a part of my life for so long, their music a source of strength during some of my darkest times. Why shouldn't they be there for one of the best days of my life, too?

So, we agreed. On our wedding day, June would sit at the front with our guests, and I — along with Terry and my granddaughter Courtney — would walk down the aisle to the space-rock sound of Hawkwind.

Looking back, I can't think of a more fitting way to begin our next chapter together.

The months ahead were filled with planning, every detail carefully arranged for what would be a truly unforgettable day.

When the moment finally arrived, the hall was packed with our guests, all waiting — not for the bride, but for the groom, his best man, and the flower girl.

At precisely 1:00 p.m., the registrar called for silence. Then, the soft, ethereal notes of **World of Tiers** from Hawkwind's **Levitation** album filled the room. With Courtney proudly leading the way, Terry and I walked confidently down the aisle.

We had written much of the ceremony ourselves, and I had the honour of reading it aloud, speaking not just for myself but for both of us, in the presence of our closest friends and family.

As part of the service, another dear friend, Davey, read a Native American wedding blessing. It was a deeply meaningful moment. The indigenous people of the North American plains had unknowingly played a profound role in my healing. Their history, their spirituality, had given me solace during my darkest days.

With our vows exchanged, we walked together back down the aisle to another Hawkwind track — this time, the hauntingly beautiful **Lost Chronicles** from the **Xenon Codex** album. It was the perfect soundtrack to an already extraordinary day.

But the surprises weren't over yet.

At the reception, as tradition dictated, Terry read aloud several wedding cards before delivering his speech. But he saved one for last.

The final card he opened wasn't just any card. It was from Hawkwind themselves — signed by each member of the band.

For me, that moment was everything. Hawkwind had not only been a source of strength during my illness, but now, in some small way, they had been part of one of the happiest days of my life.

June has always understood that Hawkwind is more than just music to me; they are a part of my story, woven into my journey. She never hesitated in supporting my wish to have them share in our wedding, even from afar. That night, as our celebration continued, I knew this was a day that would remain forever etched in our hearts.

But June also understood something else — something deeper. She knew of my connection to the Lakota people. Though they never knew it, their history, their spirit, had given me strength when I needed it most. They had offered me guidance without asking for anything in return. Years later, June herself would come to share an experience with the Lakota Oglala people, embracing the importance of their history in a way neither of us could have foreseen.

And yet, despite all this — the music, the culture, the unwavering love surrounding me — there was something I had struggled with for so long.

For much of my life, I had felt like a man lost in the shadows, weighed down by the uncertainty of my past illness. I was shrouded in self-doubt, haunted by negativity.

But on that day, something changed.

Slowly, but surely, I began to see myself clearly for the first time.

I wasn't just a survivor. I wasn't just a patient.

I was John Walker Pattison. And I was finally becoming the man I had always been.

Chapter 13
My World Falls Apart

I am neither unique nor special — countless others have faced the devastation of cancer, and, inevitably, many more will in the future. A cancer diagnosis is life-altering; it becomes a permanent part of who you are, shadowing every experience and shaping every moment. Even as you learn to cope, its presence lingers, impossible to ignore.

Even on days when it's not at the forefront of your thoughts, it remains just beneath the surface — a constant reminder of a battle fought and a reality endured. A diagnosis leaves an indelible mark, branding individuals with one of society's most feared labels. It reshapes personal philosophies, alters perspectives, and forces a re-evaluation of life's priorities.

Only now are policymakers in healthcare beginning to acknowledge that survivorship demands long-term support. For decades, those who survived cancer were expected to navigate its lasting challenges alone. This long-overdue shift toward ongoing care is a welcome change — one that recognizes not just the struggle to survive, but the need to truly live beyond the diagnosis.

No textbook can truly capture the gravity of a cancer diagnosis and its profound effects — unless, of course, the author has been personally affected. Healthcare professionals may express empathy, but they can only attempt to grasp the true weight of cancer — its power to erode sanity, influence emotions, manipulate the mind, and evoke unparalleled fear. In my view, it remains a life-altering experience unlike any other.

After heart disease, cancer is the second leading cause of death worldwide. Despite advancements in treatment and improved survival rates, a universal cure remains elusive. The word 'cancer' is still synonymous with fear — and, unfortunately, stigma. Statistics indicate that one in two people will receive a cancer diagnosis at some point in their lives, yet psychological support remains limited, though it is gradually improving.

Hodgkin lymphoma, once a deadly disease, is now often associated with a cure. However, it still claims lives, and its long-term effects, like those of other cancers, are only beginning to be fully understood. While surviving thirty or forty-years after treatment remains rare, the number of long-term survivors is growing. This will allow researchers to assess the true impact of cancer treatment over a lifetime.

So, to be a survivor for half-a-century is a humbling honour for me to carry — my shadow embellished with gratitude and pride.

Advances in early detection, targeted therapies, and more sophisticated treatments have significantly improved survival rates for many cancers. Yet, there remains an urgent need to support those who live beyond the disease. Cancer is a complex puzzle, and many pieces are still missing. Until we complete the picture, we cannot fully understand its consequences.

The risk of developing a secondary cancer due to treatment — known as carcinogenesis — remains a subject of debate. Some studies dismiss the risk, while others estimate it as low as 5% or as high as 40%. The likelihood depends on numerous factors, including the type of cancer, the treatment received, age, gender, and other variables. Research indicates that lymphoma patients, in particular, face an increased risk of developing secondary malignancies or luekaemia due to prior treatments.

As a cancer survivor of fifty-years, I was unaware of the risks associated with treatment-related secondary cancer. It simply wasn't a consideration when I underwent treatment — nor was I asked to provide consent. Today, however, patients receive far more information, and legally, they must sign a consent form before beginning treatment.

Healthcare professionals are obligated to explain both the short-term and long-term risks of treatment. With so much more information available, patients may now question whether undergoing gruelling treatment is worth the potential risk of secondary malignancies and chronic illness. Ultimately, only the patient can make that decision — but only if they have all the necessary information.

Looking back, I wonder: had I known about these risks decades ago, would I have chosen the same treatment, one that was so difficult to endure? Many people speculate about what they would do if faced with a cancer diagnosis, saying, '*If I had cancer, I would do this or that.*' To them, I say with respect: Until you are in that position, you cannot truly know how you will react.

I first learned about the risk of secondary cancer through my nursing career. The discovery hit me like a freight train. For weeks, I struggled to sleep, my mind racing with questions. The most pressing one was: '*What can I do about it now?*'

Unfortunately, not much — except to remain vigilant, monitor my body for any concerning changes, and live as healthily as possible. This is why I believe all cancer patients should receive complete and transparent information before starting treatment. Only then can they make an informed choice about their care.

Of course, this raises an ethical dilemma: should patients already burdened with a cancer diagnosis be given even more difficult information to process? How many might refuse life-saving treatment out of fear of developing another cancer or chronic illness years later?

Yet withholding this knowledge contradicts the very principles of informed consent and patient empowerment. The information is readily available online, so surely, it is better explained by a healthcare professional than left to patients to uncover on their own.

Had I been given this information all those years ago and chosen not to undergo chemotherapy, one thing is certain — I would not be here now sharing my story. The ethical debate surrounding the long-term consequences of cancer treatment will continue, as it should.

In the end, this is yet another burden cancer survivors must carry. And while it is easy to say we should not dwell on it, in reality, that is much harder to do. Research may help identify long-term health risks, but it cannot definitively determine an individual's likelihood of developing another cancer as a result of primary treatment. That uncertainty is something survivors must learn to live with.

Today, this risk is likely to be lessened due to the fact we now use more targeted therapies, such as drugs that are aimed at specific cell surface antigens, immunotherapy, and CAR T therapy (Chimeric Antigen Receptor T-Cell). Radiotherapy is much more of a targeted treatment than it was in the 1970s, which has led to some of my chronic illnesses. Needless to say, more treatments will be developed in the coming decades.

It is not my intention to scare or worry cancer survivors, surviving survivorship is hard enough, but I raise the issue primarily from a patient's perspective. It is a fact that all of this information is readily available on that wonderful medium we know as the internet; the media have also been known to print articles on the very subject occasionally, but not always accurately.

As a duty of care, I feel the health professional has an obligation to tell cancer patients about these risks to ensure that they get the facts rather than the fiction. The media are responsible for much of the scaremongering respecting cancer.

All too often we see patients portrayed in a negative light, experiencing horrendous side effects of treatment, particularly when seen on television.

Side effects these days are less severe and better controlled than a decade earlier. However, that is certainly not to say they do not occur, as that would be a foolhardy statement. Of course, they do, but the lesser side effects do not diminish from the seriousness of the disease or the harsh reality of chemotherapy.

The problem with negative portrayal is that it can cause permanent damage in the minds of the patients and their loved ones, heartache and unnecessary grief for those currently undergoing treatment. For those diagnosed with cancer and about to embark upon its treatment pathway, there is an expectation that those side effects, typically, and graphically highlighted, will definitely occur. This only serves to instil fear, and trepidation into the very minds of individuals about to receive the treatment.

Surely, this cannot be right. The media must recognize that accurate reporting is not only their responsibility but also crucial for cancer patients. I am not suggesting they avoid covering cancer-related stories of public interest. Rather, I am asking for diligence and clarity in their reporting.

Too often, the media focus on the most dramatic narratives while ignoring the many patients who undergo chemotherapy and continue working or those who experience little to no side effects. These everyday realities do not generate headlines or boost television ratings, so they are rarely reported.

Instead, the media often reinforce fear and stigma surrounding cancer, perpetuating the misconception that a diagnosis is an automatic death sentence. In reality, survival rates are improving, and advances in treatment are occurring faster than journals can publish them. The prognosis for many cancers is better than ever before, yet this progress is frequently overshadowed by sensationalism.

New drugs are constantly being developed to manage treatment side effects more effectively, improving patients' quality of life. However, what cannot be underestimated is the psychological toll of a cancer diagnosis. The media — like the medical community — must acknowledge the emotional impact of cancer and recognize that survivorship itself is a distinct health issue.

Similarly, when reporting on new chemotherapy drugs, scientific accuracy is essential. Headlines often proclaim breakthrough cures or revolutionary treatments, but upon closer examination, the reports are often misleading or exaggerated.

This type of reporting fosters false hope. Patients may read about a promising new treatment only to discover it is still in the experimental stage or not widely available. The emotional toll of such misinformation can be devastating, leading to disappointment, distress, and even a loss of trust in the healthcare system.

The media have an obligation to report advancements in cancer care, but they must do so responsibly. No one — myself included — can truly understand the heartbreak of believing in a *'miracle cure'* only to be told by a doctor that it is not an option. Unfortunately, this scenario plays out in clinical practice far too often.

We cannot play mind games with cancer patients, their state of mind is often very fragile, and such behaviour could cause further psychological trauma. In the same context, fertility issues raise various concerns for cancer patients undergoing treatment. We know which drugs cause infertility, so there is a need to be careful with the selection of the drugs used for treatments, but also, individuals about to undergo chemotherapy need to be informed of the fertility risks.

Sperm banking was never an option for me back in 1975. But as the number of long-term cancer survivors grows, we are learning that some men experience a regeneration of sperm — even decades later, sometimes more than thirty years after treatment.

The lead-up to Christmas in 1999 became a time that would forever mark both the highest and lowest points of my life, all within a matter of weeks.

June had been feeling a little off for a while — not seriously unwell, just enough to spark a suspicion. She brushed it aside, convincing herself it couldn't possibly be what she thought. Then, one evening, she came home from work, her face a mixture of nerves and joy, and shared the news: she was pregnant.

At that moment, an indescribable euphoria swept over me. There's nothing quite like the realization that you're about to become a parent. My mind instantly filled with dreams and questions. Will it be a boy or a girl? What colour should we paint the nursery? Every thought brimmed with excitement and anticipation. December 14th became a date etched in my heart — the start of a new chapter, filled with hope.

Survivorship had already given me so much, but now, life had offered me the ultimate gift: the chance to bring new life into the world.

But joy, as I would soon learn, can be heartbreakingly fleeting.

Twelve weeks later, our world came crashing down. We lost the baby to miscarriage. The devastation of that loss was unlike anything I had ever experienced — even more painful than my cancer diagnosis decades earlier. The emotional turmoil was overwhelming, a tidal wave of grief, tears, and desperation. I had never known pain like it. It felt as though the world had collapsed around me, leaving me stranded in an abyss of sorrow.

The one question I couldn't escape was why? Why could life be so cruel? But no answer ever came.

Even now, all these years later, the memory remains raw, like an open wound that never fully heals. The despair of that time became part of me, a silent ache that lingers in my heart, filled with unanswered questions and unspoken pain. It is a grief that exists in quiet moments, a sorrow that never truly fades.

It is a deafening silence within, a hidden cascade of tears for the unfulfilled dream of fatherhood.

June and I leaned heavily on each other during those dark days. Despite the love and support of family and friends — who became our lifeline, calling nightly to offer comfort and understanding — the house felt unbearably quiet. The shadows of our loss loomed large, and no amount of consolation could ease the psychological devastation.

We clung to each other, crying, reflecting, and trying to make sense of it all. Ultimately, we had to accept what we couldn't change. Nature had intervened, we told ourselves, though why remained elusive.

Through it all, I learned that grief is a deeply personal journey, one that can't be erased by words or time. Yet, the experience also underscored the strength of our love — the kind that endures through unspeakable pain and reminds us to hold on to each other when the world feels impossibly cruel.

Yes, I have adopted, and yes, I have two fabulous step-daughters who bring joy and meaning to my life. They have filled my life with love, laughter, and the kind of family connection I cherish deeply. But even so, there remains an ache that no amount of time or love can fully erase: the knowledge that my bloodline ends with me.

The realization that I will never biologically father a child is a quiet sorrow, a bittersweet companion to my journey through parenthood in other forms. It's not something I dwell on every day, but it's there, a lingering shadow in the background of an otherwise beautiful life. I celebrate the bonds I have with my daughters and the life we share, yet the unfulfilled dream of holding a child who carries my DNA is a loss that stays with me.

It is a complex mixture of gratitude and grief — a deep appreciation for the family I have built, paired with the wistful longing for what might have been. While I have come to terms with this reality, it is not without moments of reflection, when the thought of '*what if*' sneaks in, unbidden.

Still, life has a way of teaching us that love transcends biology. The connections we forge, the relationships we nurture, and the care we give —these are what truly defines family. I hold on to that truth as a source of comfort and purpose, finding joy in the here and now while honouring the dreams that have shaped me.

Tests done months later by our doctor conclusively showed that my sperm, although low, had indeed regenerated. However, now into my sixties and with additional health problems, I had to accept that the reality of biologically having a son or daughter would not happen to me, and it remains my greatest heartache.

Cancer can ensure that you reflect on every aspect of life generally, to see life without the pressure of conforming to mainstream views, to evaluate all that life has to offer and make your own decisions about it. It also causes you to reflect on your values and beliefs and, for me personally, I was confused about the dilemma of religion.

I had to admit that whilst religion is an important and powerful component for some people, it was not for me. The views expressed in this chapter are solely my views and are influenced by the experiences of what you have read so far. Importantly, they are not expressed to offend or insult anyone else's views or opinions, but to rationalize why I believe what I do.

In the same way that I do not judge anyone else on the grounds of religious belief, then equally I do not expect to be judged for the stance that I take. The ultimate questions we have all asked, and which has not yet been answered and probably never will be, is, what is the meaning of life. Where do we come from, why are we here, how did we get here and, of course, what about God, does he or she exist?

It's a dilemma that has confronted every individual, regardless of cultural or religious beliefs. When faced with a cancer diagnosis, the challenges of treatment, and the inevitable confrontation with mortality, many begin to question their faith — and understandably so.

Ultimately, the decision comes down to one simple truth: you either believe, or you do not. For those who hold onto their faith, it may even be strengthened, offering a source of comfort through difficult times. But for me, the faith I once had — before my illness and Donna's — gave way to scepticism.

There were too many questions without answers, too little evidence to convince me of God's existence. Even when I faced the prospect of an early death, I saw it not as God's will, but as a simple twist of fate — a difficult hand of cards I had been dealt. Similarly, I could not reconcile Donna's illness as part of some divine plan. It made no sense to me whatsoever.

Beyond my own experience, I struggle with the idea of a caring God when I look at the world around me — rampant poverty, disease, and the cruelty of life itself. Wars fuelled by religious ideology have been a defining part of human history, leading me to believe that religion is often either a comforting crutch or a dangerously narrow worldview.

That said, I firmly believe that faith is a personal choice, shaped by individual experience. It is not my place to criticize another person's beliefs, just as no one should impose their faith on another. In theory, we are all made the same, no person inherently better than another. As such, we owe it to one another to respect each other's values.

Sadly, the world does not operate this way. History proves that humanity is its own worst enemy when it comes to respect and coexistence. Destitution, prejudice, and hatred are all deeply embedded in societies across the world, and too often, religion is at the heart of these conflicts.

Take the so-called 'holy wars' in the Middle East — a relentless cycle of religious hatred, a tinderbox of bigotry. The compassionate core of religious philosophy has been cast aside in favour of division and hostility. Catholics and Protestants have battled for centuries in the name of faith. Across the globe, religion has fuelled some of history's most savage wars.

Wicked and unprecedented racism founded around religious doctrine, how can that be representative of religion, a so-called caring way of life? I simply do not understand that. Different religions cannot even agree on the presence of a single God. It is a sad fact that we live in a fragmented world. I guess 9/11 is the prime example of religious hatred.

An attack of such magnitude and destruction that mere words could never describe the pain and torment it caused — all founded around an ideology of hatred that identifies the west as the enemy. And yet, just look at the unity that came from that dreadful assault. Admittedly, some people get their solace from their religion, and I would never belittle that fact.

I suppose that's the weakness of mankind. The earth has been around for billions of years and thousands of Gods have been worshipped before the current one, who is to say that another won't take his or her place in the next millennium. There is no definitive proof that there is such a thing as God, yet people choose to believe it, in hope, but also in the fear of not being welcomed into his utopia.

Religion has not always been there. It was created, and evolved over the centuries, as a tool to control the people — to wield a power that the people feared. If we destroyed all the religious textbooks, and, also destroyed all the scientific text — when they are re-written, the science would be the same because it is based on fact, and is provable. However, the religious textbooks would look entirely different, as they are based on anecdotal stories, not fact.

I have little doubt that there was such a person as Jesus, was he the son of God? I think not, but, that is just my opinion. Furthermore, the bible is littered with contradiction and I, personally, believe it has been grossly exaggerated over the years and much of this is to support the strength and hold that the church has over people. So many of the stories in the bible were written years, often hundreds of years, after the events they describe. Many Biblical teachings, and indeed, doctrines conflict with the majority of scientific thought.

Religion does not encourage individuals to ask the questions I pose here, quite the contrary. Significantly and before my own and indeed, Donna's illness, I did believe in a God, although I was never a fervent supporter. I guess like so many, it was a fear of denouncing a God in case there was such an entity and the risk of being denied at the end of life.

For many, myself included, it is the experience of life that will mould personal or philosophical beliefs. If God is the creator of the earth, why is it that the planet is so unpredictable, where is his calming influence, his power? Violent earthquakes and hurricanes, tsunamis and weather out of our control and which most often affects the Third World. That's a caring creator? Not in my view and ironically, these elements that are so destructive to innocent life are referred to as 'Acts of God.'

It is my understanding that religion is supposed to bring people together with a forgiving and compassionate ethos, yet the world over; religion proves divisive, confrontational and causes segregation across all the different sects and beliefs.

Shouldn't all religious believers be united and worship the same God, or is that too simplistic?

Science can now explain and more importantly prove the origins of life and the evolution of the universe, formed by the merging of gases and minerals 13.8 billion years ago. Physics explains that within the universe there are many hundreds of different galaxies and many of these may be capable of supporting life.

To me, religion simply does not stand up to scrutiny and analysis. Life is too short for any approach other than mutual respect. Enjoy it while you can, for if you don't, one day, it'll be too late. That said, I do not intend to sound *'Holier than thou,'* nor do I believe that I am judgemental, I have my views and opinions on many things as we all do; neither do I think that any of my actions over the years have been taken in a deliberate attempt to hurt anyone.

I firmly believe that we are all entitled to the freedom of speech without fear of retribution. I live every day the only way I know, grateful for every day as it comes around, knowing that I am fortunate to be alive and passionate about my music, my work, and my family life; I love my wife unreservedly and look forward to the future ahead, although unsure as to what it holds.

The hatred inflicted on the world by religion is unfathomable, beyond its ethos. It is about time that the world's community, lifted their eyes, and try to establish world peace. Now, there's a challenge!

My views expressed in this chronicle are not intended to upset or offend; they truly represent how cancer has manipulated my thought processes and my ideals. And again, I would clarify, that I have nothing against religion, each to their own, and I respect other people's right to believe in what they believe.

Chapter 14
Ten Seconds of Forever

My journey was a profound one, each stage contributing layers of depth and an understanding to who I was, and have now become. It started with my musical discovery, and Hawkwind. But, my mind opened up to broader perspectives, including a deep respect for the Lakota Sioux Nation, their wisdom, spirituality, and their survival instincts. From there, facing the immense challenge of a cancer diagnosis, and the psychological battle I almost lost — but, resulted in an unparalleled personal growth. Recognition of life's duality, its beauty, innocence, and its difficulties — a unique kind of wisdom that only my deep, and transformative experience could elicit.

I acknowledged that as a cancer patient, a coping mechanism was essential. Everyone copes in different ways and Hawkwind and the Lakota Sioux proved to be my coping mechanisms and without them, I would have struggled. Equally, and as importantly, my family were my building blocks of support.

Throughout the whole journey, I tried to discover myself, someone I had not known until that moment — yet, I remained uncertain as to my true identity. It then continued with the harsh and abrasive reality of being the parent of a child struck down by cancer, the destructive essence of coming close to losing your child to the predatory enemy of leukaemia. The desperation and helplessness that only a parent can know.

The joy and gratitude of survivorship from both perspectives and then the role of a student nurse and the ascendancy to senior haematology clinical nurse specialist, a unique and most importantly, privileged rotation. I had travelled full circle, from the patient to the prescriber of chemotherapy, an ironic twist of fate.

But my life is not, by any stretch of the imagination, over yet, it continues today, as the ever-youthful Hawkwind still actively tour regularly, fuelling my travels around the country; travelling to a gig in Belfast and to the next in Manchester, from Newcastle to London and everywhere in between.

From 1975 to the present, life has been an incredible journey — one of discovery, transformation, and profound realization. No work of fiction could ever match the depth and intensity of this experience. Among the many defining moments, my journey with cancer stands out as one that reshaped my beliefs, philosophy, and entire outlook on life. The raw reality of this experience has left an indelible mark, forever changing the way I see the world and my place within it.

I've now travelled three hundred and sixty degrees and although the future can never be considered absolutely certain, my fate is already mapped out in front of me. What further surprises will the '*shadow of a survivor*' hold? Well, quite a few it seems.

Time stands still for no man and there is one important question that never goes away, particularly as the years march on, a question that frequently navigates my deep inner thoughts. Even after fifty years and despite my pragmatism or my own logical thought processes, the question remains, will it ever come back?

Perhaps it's because of the work that I did, or possibly, it is due to the new sense of security and happiness I have found with June that this question is now more prominent in my mind than ever before. 2004 was a significant year; in August, I re-married and walked down the aisle to the sound of Hawkwind.

Then, at the annual Hawkwind Christmas concert at London's Astoria, I got an invitation to the band's after-show party. And, eventually, after a thirty-three-year wait, I finally met and chatted with the man who for all that time had been my best friend, yet in all of that time I had never had the privilege of meeting; Dave Brock, founding member of Hawkwind.

In 2006, Hawkwind held a three-day festival at Donnington Park when I was invited onto the stage during their performance to recite '**Ten Seconds of Forever**,' a piece of work the band had written for their album Space Ritual back in 1972. However, I had re-written the lyrics to reflect the first ten seconds of a cancer diagnosis:

In the tenth second of forever
I was informed that my world would end and with it my very existence
In the ninth second of forever
I felt a numbness overcome my body, the tingling sensation of fear and
the chronic pain of this reality
In the eighth second of forever
I thought of a leaf, a stone and the creaking branches of the ancient
oak tree and the innocence of life
In the seventh second of forever

I remembered an empty room where voices spoke to me about nothing
In the sixth second of forever
I thought of the life I would not lead and the effects of my confused
mind
In the fifth second of forever
I thought of the toxic poison that would attack my fragile veins
In the fourth second of forever
I could remember nothing, I did not love
In the third second of forever
I thought of my Father, my Mother, and my sister crying
In the penultimate second of my diagnosis
I saw the rain caressing the window, the marshmallow clouds drift
through the sky
In the first and final second of what seemed forever
I thought of the others, those that had not been so fortunate and the
long past that had led to now
And never, never forever...

It was an incredible experience standing in front of over 800 people, and moreover, my wife June was at the side of the stage to see it. I received many compliments afterwards from people I did and did not know.

Only a few months after my performance on stage with Hawkwind I plucked up the courage to ask the band's manager about joining the band on their next tour as part of the road crew. She pondered for less than a few moments and said yes.

Subsequently, I spent two tours (2007 & 2008) on the road with Hawkwind selling merchandise, unloading and setting up for gigs and stripping the stage after the gig was finished. I was on the road in the tour bus with other roadies, and of course, the band members. Fate can be a wonderful thing.

I was now musically inspired to form a band of my own, although I had never played an instrument in my life. I bought a synthesizer, then a keyboard, then another keyboard until eventually, I got Robin on guitar, Matt on Bass, Vince on vocals and Richard on drums.

Naturally, we played 'Space Rock' and were called 'Wind of Change.' As a result of my links with the band, we were invited to support Hawkwind at a three-day festival in Devon. Standing proudly on stage with my musical friends and hearing the sound of my keyboards echo through the air was a breathtaking reflection of where I had been over the past decades.

After three years of playing with *'Wind of Change,'* the guys went off to pursue other musical interests. But, I was just getting started on a musical pathway and, therefore, I decided to continue as a solo artist, calling myself *'The Weird Noise Master,'* because of the sound I was aiming to create. A mixture of psychedelic rock combined with very early Pink Floyd with the added influence of Hawkwind.

I played locally for a few years until my good friend Alan Davey, who was perhaps one of the most influential bass players Hawkwind had ever had, invited me to support his band *'The Psychedelic Warlords'* on a national tour. Alan is one of the most talented musicians I know and is destined for mega-stardom in the near future.

After touring with Alan through England and Scotland, I hung up my keyboards with a deep sense of satisfaction. Alan now lives near Death Valley and we remain good friends.

Yes, life was good, but then the timely reminder that I was still surviving survivorship came in late 2008. Following some routine investigations, the discovery of a tumour on my bowel wall took me by surprise. It was surgically removed and thankfully found to be benign.

But, the following year, I required a series of investigations which determined that because of the treatment given to me so many years earlier, my Pituitary gland was now no longer functioning as it should, a condition called, Hypopituitarism. The result of this underactive Pituitary gland is that I now have osteoporosis, and a higher risk of heart disease or even a brain tumour. Consequently, I now require daily hormone treatment, in addition to calcium and vitamin D supplementation.

In the same year, I discovered a small growth on my abdomen which, after an investigation, was found to be a secondary cancer caused by the salubrious Radiotherapy treatment I received way back in 1976; this was easily removed by surgical excision and never caused a problem again.

Later in 2009, my beloved Newcastle United endured relegation from the Premier League. Thankfully, they secured automatic promotion the following season. Meanwhile, in the same year, ex-England, and ex-Newcastle United manager (although he managed many other clubs, including the mighty

Barcelona), and importantly, an all-round lovely man, Sir Bobby Robson lost his fight with lung cancer.

The journey of survivorship often comes with its share of bittersweet realities, and timely reminders that I was far from invincible and the treatment that was given decades earlier was still influencing my life. Following a rapid onset of breathlessness, a chest x-ray revealed that I had a condition called Pulmonary Fibrosis, a condition whereby the lungs are scarred and breathing is more difficult.

The respiratory consultant told me that this was the lingering impact of past Radiotherapy, which underscores the reality that even victories in health come with their own set of challenges. This may become more debilitating over the years; as a result, my inhaler is never far from reach!

Yet despite this legacy, I have achieved so many unexpected milestones and firmly believe that life truly is sweet, and I realize that I am lucky to be here and appreciate each day as it happens. But I want more!

It is very true to say that we all need motivation in our lives, and I was no exception. Hawkwind offered me their music which took me to another dimension and an abandonment of reality, an escapism that I required on many an occasion.

Yet, it was the Lakota Sioux who had inadvertently taken me under their 'Star Quilt' and comforted me like one of their own. My respect and admiration for a people so exploited, so maligned and so very nearly destroyed was a solace I will carry with me forever and is beyond my full appreciation.

Despite my love for my work, I understood the fleeting nature of life, the certainty that one day it would be my last. So, in 2012, I chose flexible retirement, reducing my hours to just twenty. Aware of my health's fragility, I sought to embrace the finer things — our grandchildren, fishing, photography, and, most significantly, travel.

Travel, especially to America, has always been vital for June and me. We have explored many corners of the world, yet something about the vast, storied landscapes of the United States continually draws us back. As a reward to myself following retirement, we planned a three-week trip, beginning in Arizona — naturally taking in the Grand Canyon, the fabled town of Tombstone, and beyond. But the true highlight would be South Dakota, where, at last, I would stand upon the hallowed ground of Wounded Knee.

Words fail to fully capture what that meant to me.

We had chosen a boutique bed and breakfast in Rapid City, and the drive to Wounded Knee was just over an hour. That Tuesday morning, golden sunlight poured across the rolling hills as we left the city behind, giving the landscape a quiet majesty. The prairie stretched endlessly before us, its overwhelming greenness exuding a solemn, almost sacred stillness.

It was a drive filled with anticipation, yet more than that, a drive of solitude and reflection.

Upon arriving, we pulled off the road, stepping into history. Almost instantly, two Lakota elders approached us, their sun-baked, timeworn faces bearing witness to generations past. With quiet dignity, they offered us their hand-made trinkets, welcoming us warmly to Wounded Knee. Their presence was humbling. They had no idea who I was, where I had been, what I had experienced, or how deeply their history and culture resonated within me.

After purchasing their beautiful crafts and exchanging kind farewells, we turned toward the red, dusty path leading to the entrance of Wounded Knee Creek Cemetery. My anticipation swelled with each step, sending a shiver from the top of my spine to the soles of my feet — goose bumps upon goose bumps.

Wounded Knee was everything I had envisioned. Not a grand, sweeping expanse, but a place of profound stillness. A sacred ground of sorrow and reverence. Ancient graves lay scattered, their wooden crosses weathered by time. Headstones bore names I instantly recognized — among them, Chief Big Foot.

It was not just a resting place. It was a whispered history, an unbroken spirit, a paradise in its own way.

For someone who had openly rejected religion, a strange and undeniable sense of spirituality filled the air around me. It was an honour beyond words to walk upon the sacred ground of the Lakota Oglala people, paying my respects to the fallen warriors who had perished there.

I stood in that solemn field where, on December 29, 1890, three hundred and fifty men, women, and children were mercilessly massacred by the Seventh Cavalry. The weight of history pressed down upon me — grief, anger, and reverence intertwining in an almost overwhelming tide of emotion. And yet, despite the sorrow, I felt privileged beyond measure to stand upon the hallowed earth of the Lakota Sioux.

Humbled beyond words to call the Lakota people, my friends.

Since that first visit, June and I have returned many times, making what became a sacred pilgrimage. Until my last breath, I will never feel more at peace, more at home, than I do on that land. Surviving survivorship was, at last, revealing its rewards.

2018 was a year of profound highs and lows. Forty-three years after my cancer diagnosis, I decided to reach out to the Pine Ridge Indian Reservation Council, seeking permission to visit the reservation itself. After weeks of correspondence, I received an invitation that left me speechless — a council member extended an offer for me to spend a week as a guest of the Lakota Sioux.

My humble soul could scarcely believe it. Fate had carried me from the mind of a young, naïve adolescent — one who found solace in the history of the Sioux Nation — to this moment, where I would physically stand upon their sacred land — among them as a guest.

My guide for the week was Collins Gay, a Lakota Oglala native in his mid-fifties. This journey, unlike the others, I would make alone — a week of exploration across the vast expanse of the reservation, to places few white men had ever seen. Among them, the grave of one of the greatest Lakota leaders of all time, Chief Red Cloud.

Pine Ridge Indian Reservation is the poorest in America. Unemployment hovers between 80 and 95 percent. Life expectancy is a mere 52 years for women, and just 48 years for men. I had seen poverty before, but nothing like this. And yet, amidst the hardship, I found an unshakable pride that outshone the disparity.

They called me brother. They called me friend.

And, most significantly, they called me 'Wasi'chu' — meaning, 'non-native.' or simply 'white man.'

On my final night at the reservation, I was honoured with an invitation to speak before the Oglala Sioux Tribe (OST) Council. I thanked them with all the sincerity in my heart, especially Collins, whose kindness had guided me through this journey.

Then, something happened that left me utterly undone.

Before I could take my leave, the council presented me with a Star Quilt. I was flabbergasted — speechless, my eyes welling with tears. The quilt's intricate design, inspired by the morning star, carried a deep and sacred meaning. It was the last and brightest star on the eastern horizon before dawn, a symbol of the spirits' journey to earth, a connection between the living and those who had passed.

In that moment, I felt the weight of their history, their generosity, and their unbreakable spirit. And for the first time, I truly understood what it meant to be embraced by the Lakota people.

Today, Star Quilts remain one of the most treasured gifts of the Lakota Sioux, draped over the shoulders of recipients as a symbol of protection on their journey through life — bestowed only upon honoured guests. Historically, these quilts adorned the warriors and hunters of the Lakota as they returned from battle or a successful hunt. And in that deeply reflective, poignant moment, I realized that, in many ways, I too had been in a battle of my own.

I was honoured. I was humbled, most importantly, I was speechless!

When the speaker announced that I was now an honorary member of the tribal council, I was overwhelmed. A higher honour, I could not imagine. Tears streamed down my face.

As I left Pine Ridge Indian Reservation that evening — Monday, May 21, 2018 — ironically, exactly forty-three years to the day since I began chemotherapy, the setting sun cast a golden glow across the horizon. I felt a torrent of emotions: pride, gratitude, humility. But above all else, I made myself a promise — one day, I would return to my friends of the Sioux Nation, to the resilient people of Pine Ridge Indian Reservation.

Today, I travel across the North of England, and occasionally beyond, sharing the story of the Lakota Sioux — their history, their exploitation, and their ongoing struggle.

Our trips to America continue, as does our growing family. Among all our journeys, one stands above the rest — Montana. If heaven had an earthly counterpart, I am certain it would be there. Had I been twenty years younger and in better health, June and I would have undoubtedly made a home in Livingston, Montana, or perhaps Rapid City, South Dakota.

To date, we have been blessed with five grandchildren and one great-grandson. After the birth of our youngest grandson, Daniel, I had no idea how significant he would become, nor the support he would unknowingly provide. Little did I know how soon I would need it?

We had planned a short holiday to Washington, D.C., bringing twenty-one-month-old Daniel along with us. The day before departure, I noticed a single speck of blood in my urine. It could have been something serious — or nothing at all. Rather than let it interfere with our trip, I scheduled an appointment with my doctor for our return and pushed the worry aside.

The following day, we jetted off across the Atlantic.

I saw no further signs of blood — until I used the toilet on the aircraft. A red stream, and I knew instinctively what it meant.

Throughout our visit to D.C., every trip to the bathroom confirmed my worst fears. Yet, strangely, I felt no pain — only a growing sense of unease. My biggest concern wasn't my health, but the possibility of a major urinary issue while still in the States and the overwhelming financial burden that could bring.

Safely back home, my GP issued a two-week referral. At Newcastle Freeman Hospital, a catheter was passed into my bladder, revealing a tumour. Still, it would be another three weeks before I would learn whether it was benign or malignant.

Those three weeks were pure hell.

The tumour had been removed, but the procedure had damaged my prostate, leaving me in agonizing pain. Each attempt to pass water was torture. I depended on powerful painkillers — liquid morphine among them — which, in turn, left me severely constipated, only amplifying my suffering.

By the time I returned to Freeman Hospital, I already knew the answer.

Buried deep in my consciousness, the truth had long settled. Decades earlier, during my initial treatment, I had received high doses of Cyclophosphamide — a drug known to be urotoxic. There could only be one conclusion.

Bladder cancer!

It could be said that I was calmer for this consultation than any other in my life, despite anticipating the result. Given the treatment I had received, I knew I faced an increased risk of secondary cancer — particularly bowel, lung, leukaemia, or lymphoma.

With that in mind, I felt that the news could have been much worse. Not wanting to be flippant or dismissive of the seriousness of any malignant diagnosis, I understood that bladder cancer, if caught early, is relatively treatable — though not without its challenges, including the discomfort and embarrassment of the personal nature of the examinations. And so, I went in, and the diagnosis I had expected was confirmed.

As for treatment, the tumour had already been surgically removed, and chemotherapy had been instilled into the bladder. Beyond that, all that remained were regular cystoscopy tests, all of which, up until 2023, have been clear. My journey on the road to surviving survivorship would continue.

Today, the prognosis for lymphoma and other cancers is far more favourable than it was in the 1970s. However, we must remember that cancer, including bladder cancer, still claims lives. While chemotherapy has become much more refined and its side effects better managed, navigating treatment remains a difficult road — physically, and without a doubt, psychologically.

Unfortunately, even in today's modern healthcare system, stigma and misconceptions about cancer and its treatments persist. Many anticipate only negativity and debilitating side effects, when in reality; drug dosages are now carefully calculated to minimize toxicities. Anti-nausea and supportive medications have improved dramatically, and healthcare professionals now offer a level of guidance and reassurance that was unheard of fifty years ago.

Access to written information about all aspects of cancer management is now a fundamental right of patients. Having this knowledge empowers individuals to make informed decisions, giving them a sense of control in an otherwise uncertain experience. A cancer diagnosis, however, remains a uniquely personal journey — one that affects each of us differently. Yet, the one unifying truth is that it irrevocably changes our perception of life.

Looking back, I realize that my cancer journey was not only a difficult road to navigate but also a transformative one. It allowed me to mature, to embrace life more fully, and to find appreciation in moments often taken for granted. Through reflection, I have come to value resilience, gratitude, and the undeniable strength that emerges from adversity. Ultimately, cancer shaped me, but it did not define me.

Undoubtedly, in my opinion, the cancer journey that I undertook all those years ago was not only a difficult road to navigate. It also allowed me to mature personally, to respect and enjoy life and improve my quality of life through reflection, appreciation and understanding.

Furthermore, the traumatic pain of witnessing Donna suffer at the hands of an impartial disease, indiscriminate in its choice of person, left me helpless to help my child. But Donna's ability to adjust and learn to live with her disease and take from it positivism and that a cancer diagnosis does not automatically mean a death sentence — was pivotal and influential in my philosophy.

Cancer does not have to be solely a negative experience. While coming to terms with it and enduring the hardships of the disease can be profoundly challenging, it is important to recognize the positive strides being made. More support and resources are available today than ever before, which is undeniably a step in the right direction.

At the same time, I fully appreciate and deeply respect that not everyone diagnosed with cancer will be as fortunate as Donna and I have been. Each person embarks on a unique journey, and some face outcomes that may feel insurmountable. My hope is that, one day, every person touched by cancer will have the opportunity to experience the gift of survivorship. Until then, we continue to hold space for hope, progress, and compassion for all who are on this path.

When the cancer patient has completed treatment, they are seen at regular intervals in a clinic and the longer they stay in remission, the greater the time interval between clinic visits. If discharged from follow up, they are bound to suddenly feel more vulnerable due to an associated absence of support. Cancer patients, particularly long-term survivors, are entitled to more support and the current system is changing to try to meet those demands.

Today, more and more individuals do survive the cancer experience, an acknowledgement of the advances medical science has made in respect to treatment approaches. As the survival curve becomes more acute, then the health service needs to make provision for the psychological care requirements of those of us who are called survivors.

Communication is at the heart of psychological care and to deliver that fundamental aspect of care, professionals must learn to develop closer relationships with cancer patients. Following on from my diagnosis, it was clear that many nurses and doctors would actively distance themselves from cancer patients, fearing confronting their mortality.

However, when Donna was diagnosed, the approach, although still far from perfect, was so much better than my experience in the seventies. Health care professionals, particularly the nurses, would often communicate with honesty and sincerity, no matter what question was asked, whether that question was asked by a child or a parent.

Cancer patients deserve to be supported through what is ultimately a challenge to their very existence; the most appropriate support health care providers can offer is through transparency and good communication that can increase the satisfaction of care and provide a trusting and emotional relationship.

Survivorship is sometimes just as difficult to deal with as the actual diagnosis, there is difficulty predicting what the future holds as cancer is such an unpredictable entity. In my opinion, the emotional fear that it evokes does not disappear, even after the all-clear has been given. Psychological morbidity can debilitate an individual in the same way and occasionally worse than the physical symptoms activated by cancer and its unforgiving treatment.

Psychological support is such an important component of care for any cancer patient that health care professionals ignore it at their peril. Psychological care is a lifelong need for cancer survivors; it needs to be a core component of the planned care pathway.

Today, my memory is not as good as it once was, a hidden legacy of the beneficial treatment I received decades earlier. Many of us experience brain fog at some point in our lives; however, it is both a short-term and long-term consequence of chemotherapy or radiotherapy. It manifests as a feeling of tiredness or disorientation or a distraction, or, taking an extended period to fulfil a task or an inability to concentrate on a new skill.

The engines of emotion are constantly fuelled by my doubt and worry concerning my health and long-term survival. Yes, not a day goes by, when I do not fully appreciate how fortunate I am and, yet, it is a constant battle to control these emotions. Thankfully, I have June, who is my lifeline to normality; always there to top up my glass.

Like all other individuals whose life has been affected by a cancer diagnosis, my journey was a unique one, and yet it touched more than just my life. My diagnosis was not mine alone, it belonged to everyone important to me, and it touched them almost as much as it touched me.

From those early days of my diagnosis and indeed, soon afterwards, it was thought that the entity that is lymphoma would terminate my existence, proving a wholly destructive experience. The unequalled fear of losing Donna was an experience that simple words could not come close to describing. Yet, there is no doubt that my personal profile has been enhanced by the experience of a cancer diagnosis and as the parent of a child with cancer.

As for my support, June, the love of my life, is my number one passion; throughout my cancer journey and beyond, during my darkest moments, Hawkwind were there at the end of a stylus or in concert and the Lakota Sioux unknowingly gave me the spiritual support that only those indigenous natives could; however, my family were the rocks that I depended upon even though I wrongly hid so much from them.

So what has been my magical formula in life? Naturally, there is not one single factor or component that can claim to be the reason I overcame my cancer. For me as an individual, there were many reasons, not least of these was the support and love from my family and despite their attempts at misguided, but well-intentioned, collusion, I would not be here today without them.

The inspiration and time held dreams that Hawkwind gave me without taking anything in return; the doctors and nurses whose dedication and commitment to my cause was unswerving; my Lakota companions whom I knew personally but had never met. My friends who became an extension of my family, looking out for me and accepting and cajoling me through some dark moments, you all know who you are.

My positive mental attitude focussed my attention on the fact that this was a life-threatening illness and, yet, there were times when I was emotionally unstable and bereft of happiness as the positive mentality proved an impossible direction to steer. But almost paradoxically, I felt that unhappiness and depression was an important release valve.

Despite the urges of so many to insist and plead that I maintain the '*think positive attitude*,' it is sometimes easier said than done. Further, I firmly believe that cancer patients are entitled to feel sorry for themselves from time to time. Significantly, I'm also convinced that most, if not all, would agree that a '*positive attitude*' is a major ingredient when it comes to fighting cancer.

In contrast, Donna's illness was so much harder to accept and contend with. My helplessness and sense of inadequacy when she needed me most was enormous, not knowing at that moment that what she was receiving throughout her cancer experience was something that could not be bought, love!

A transference of a sense of being wanted, being special and unique, as all children are. Strangely, her reciprocation to me as her father gave her a purpose in life. Yet even so, throughout her illness, it was as if I was in a parallel universe, unable to alleviate her suffering or ease her burden.

Everyone copes differently with a cancer diagnosis, no one element is above all others and my story is no different in that respect and as such, it is not intended to be prescriptive or a specific guide to others. It has allowed me to appreciate what many take for granted, to reflect on my mistakes and there have been many and no doubt there will be many more.

Most importantly, it allowed me to discover myself and live life to the full and enjoy every day as it happened. One day will be my last and, therefore, I would rather not have any regrets about how I lived it. Even so, like everyone, I still have dreams.

Take from my experience whatever you choose, criticize it where you feel necessary, but always remember that this was my experience of cancer as an individual, as a parent and as a senior cancer nurse specialist. I truly believe it has made me the person I am today, a better person, philosophical, caring and determined to make a difference somewhere.

Moreover, when ultimately my time is at an end on this plane, my one wish is that I am heralded into the funeral service to a Lakota sound. A fitting tribute to what, in my opinion, has been a fulfilled existence.

In my nursing career, I have won many accolades both locally and nationally. Yet, the gratitude of the patients I cared for is worth more than any prize offered by the establishment, and I know that I have been privileged to have worked in cancer services my entire nursing career. Touching the lives of so many, yet, being touched by, so many is a humbling experience that I will always cherish.

Continuing on my highway of survival, what new challenges would cross my path? In 2020, forty-five years after my diagnosis, many more individuals became survivors; survivors of an international health crisis, Covid-19. A virus that ripped the heart out of our economy, divided families, prevented grandparents from seeing their grandchildren and created an untold mental health burden for thousands, leading to an increase in suicide rates.

However, it also halted cancer treatments, which sadly contributed to mortality rates. It caused unprecedented psychological distress to thousands of cancer patients, who worried about their futures.

At the time of writing, an estimated 2.5 million people are living with cancer in the UK, and this is anticipated to rise to four million by 2030; half of those individuals diagnosed with cancer in England and Wales will survive their illness for ten years or longer, which is great news — but we still need to strive for further survival success.

Cancer continues to be a leading cause of death in this country, and with an ageing population, that means the incidence will continue to rise. Clearly, we now need a national initiative that can support the survivors of cancer, and address the psychological needs that they will shoulder for the remainder of their lives.

Chapter 15
Helping Yourself

In 2019, when I was diagnosed with Bladder cancer (the ninth most common cancer in the world), I took it in my stride. My life was in a good place, and I knew that in the greater scheme of things, there were many worse case scenarios I could have faced.

Once the surgery had taken place, and the chemotherapy instillation was complete, I felt confident of moving forward, even though I knew that the health service guidance (NICE), suggested that follow up with a cystoscopy was important. Repeat cystoscopies occurred at three, nine, and eighteen months, and then once a year thereafter, for a five-year period. The guidance also recommended discharge after five years on the assumption of being cancer free.

My follow-ups went smoothly, until in October 2023, and my penultimate cystoscopy. An aggressive recurrence was identified on two areas of the bladder wall – I was gutted!

It was subsequently decided that the most appropriate approach would be the use of laser treatment, called, *TULA* (Trans Urethral Laser Ablation). Therefore, a few weeks later, I attended Newcastle Freeman Hospital, and the procedure was undertaken.

Today, I am once again undergoing a cystoscopy surveillance programme.

Irrespective, of my ongoing health problems, attributable to the previous chemotherapy, and radiotherapy I received in the seventies — my life remains on course. Although it is a fact that my life will always be defined by my earlier cancer diagnosis. It has, and will, influence the remainder of my days.

There are moments in life when the past seems like a distant, almost surreal dream. Reflecting back, I often have to pinch myself to grasp the weight of what the past fifty years have meant. Not just the fifty years since my diagnosis, but also the forty years since my daughter, Donna — tragically, only four-year-old at the time, was diagnosed with leukaemia. Yet, she, too, would win her battle. In the face of immense uncertainty, we survived, though I am frequently reminded of those who have not — when I face up to that reality, I am saddened, yet paradoxically, grateful for my survival.

My survival, my daughter's survival, and my career in cancer services have all been the product of a journey shaped by pain, resilience, and I believe, fate. This, ultimately, has given me, an enduring gratitude for the gift of life, although it wasn't always the case. Despite my dark moments today — my best friend, my wife, June, must take a lot of the credit for the wonderful life we enjoy.

I am saddened at the fact not everyone survivors a cancer diagnosis, saddened, that my cancer diagnosis almost pushed me into permanent self-destruction. Yet, grateful for my existence and the remarkable life I have today, and an appreciation for the exemplarity career I enjoyed, exclusively, in cancer services — all of which, I believe, is because of fate.

The concept of fate is not something that everyone will embrace. However, in my view, fate mapped out my pathway, leaving me with little option other than to follow that trajectory. Over the span of fifty years, my life unfolded in unexpected directions, shaped by circumstances beyond my control.

My initial diagnosis was a turning point, marking the beginning of a profound emotional toll. I was thrust into a journey where darkness often felt insurmountable. As I navigated multiple failed treatment plans, each setback added to the weight I carried, testing my resilience in ways I had never imagined.

There were moments when hope seemed elusive, and the turmoil within me reached a breaking point. It was during this period of intense struggle that I was introduced to palliative chemotherapy. Although not a cure, it became the unexpected bridge that allowed me to move forward, easing some burdens and granting me the strength to confront the future.

In the end, fate's hand guided me through a complex and often painful journey, but it also revealed a path that allowed me to find moments of clarity and peace amidst the chaos.

Cancer remains an emotive subject, particularly for those touched by its outstretched tentacles. There are over one hundred different cancers known to medicine, yet, thanks to early detection and new treatments, more people are living longer with cancer. More people than ever before are joining me on the road, as a cancer survivor.

Living with the legacy of cancer is not always easy. However, it is the best option I have, yet, that privilege is not available, sadly, to everyone. We know, only too well, that not everyone who gets a cancer diagnosis will survive.

Importantly, there is now more support for cancer patients than ever before. In the 1970s, few nurses or doctors would discuss emotional or psychological support with patients. However, I am not complaining about that, as I understand that cancer survival rates were far less favourable at the time. Therefore, the focus was often solely on physical treatment, with little time for addressing the mental toll.

I also believe that many nurses and doctors were themselves fearful of confronting their own mortality. As a defensive mechanism, they would typically deflect the critical questions that cancer patients naturally ask. It was a difficult and emotionally charged environment, both for the patients and the healthcare providers.

Thankfully, the healthcare system has since evolved to recognize the importance of both physical and psychological support. There are now dedicated services, therapies, and support systems designed to help patients cope with the emotional side of their journey.

Critically, despite this progress, there remains a cohort of doctors and nurses in particular, who are still hesitant to engage with the deep, often uncomfortable questions posed by those undergoing cancer treatments. While the system has made great strides, this reluctance highlights the ongoing need for training and emotional support within the caregiving community itself.

Despite the many advances in survival rates, better treatment options, and improved diagnostic techniques that allow for earlier detection, the ultimate question remains: can we influence our ability to fight a cancer diagnosis and improve survival rates further?

It is a daunting thought, especially given the statistic that one in two people will receive a cancer diagnosis at some point in their lives — a frightening reality that no one can deny.

When faced with a cancer diagnosis, many of us wonder: What can we do, personally, to improve our chances of survival? While evidenced-based treatments remain the cornerstone of care, exploring complementary therapies can be empowering, and potentially, beneficial. But, whatever steps we take, they must work hand in hand with evidence-based treatments.

My chronicle of survivorship is not about making people feel guilty about their life choices, but years of research has shown that around a dozen cancers are linked to obesity, and about sixteen different cancers are caused by smoking. A suboptimal diet accounts for approximately five percent of cancers, and socio-economic disparities contribute to thousands of additional cases annually, with survival rates worse for the most deprived groups.

While my story is meant to inspire anyone touched by a cancer diagnosis, and not serve as a scientific journal, I do feel it is important to discuss risk factors and what we know about foods that may help. Though I cannot, and will not claim that certain foods can stop or reverse cancer progression, research suggests that some foods have potential cancer-fighting properties.

It is also heart-breaking to acknowledge, because of man's short-sightedness, that vast portions of the Amazon rainforest, which may have held life-changing drugs derived from its unique plant species, have been lost. Nevertheless, I believe it is critical to explore how nature can assist us in our fight against cancer.

I hope that by sharing my experience, I can offer inspiration, and highlight the importance of combining nature's resources with medical advancements in the ongoing battle against cancer. Here I present some recognized foods that potentially can help us.

Importantly, I do not make any specific claim that these can cure any type of cancer.

But, a balanced diet rich in specific nutrients can play a significant role in reducing the risk of cancer.

Berries; are nutritional powerhouses, rich in vitamins, fibre, and antioxidants such as anthocyanins, and resveratrol. These compounds, found in their vibrant blue, purple, and red pigments, may help protect the digestive tract, and support overall health.

Cruciferous Vegetables; such as broccoli, cauliflower, bok choy, cabbage, and Brussels sprouts are packed with indole-3-carbinol, a compound known for its cancer-fighting properties. Regular consumption of these vegetables is linked to a reduced risk of various cancers.

Oily Fish; salmon, tuna, and anchovies are rich in omega-3 fatty acids, which reduce inflammation and protect against breast and colorectal cancers.

Nuts; are a rich source of healthy fats, antioxidants, and other nutrients that may contribute to cancer prevention. Walnuts, in particular, are praised by the American Institute for Cancer Research for their cancer-fighting properties.

Legumes; beans, lentils, and chickpeas are nutrient-dense powerhouses rich in vitamins, minerals, protein, and fibre. They contain flavonoids; strong antioxidants that help prevent cancer.

Dark chocolate; high-cocoa-content dark chocolate is a surprising source of fibre, antioxidants, and minerals. The polyphenols and catechins in cocoa beans promote healthy gut bacteria and may lower cancer risk. However, due to its high calorie content, it's best enjoyed in moderation.

Whole Grains; such as oats, brown rice, and whole wheat, are loaded with protective antioxidants like vitamin E. Eating whole grains regularly is linked to a lower risk of at least 18 types of cancer, including colorectal cancer.

Carotenoids; the dark, leafy vegetables such as spinach and kale, act as antioxidants that help the body defend against breast, bladder, and lung cancers.

Cultured and Fermented Foods; yogurt, kefir, kombucha, and kimchi, are rich in probiotics, which boost immune function and may prevent colorectal cancer by neutralizing potential carcinogens.

Garlic; contains allicin, a sulphur compound that inhibits cancer progression. Eating garlic regularly has been linked to a lower risk of colorectal cancer. For maximum benefit, let chopped or crushed garlic sit for 15 minutes before cooking to release its active compounds.

Ginseng; a 2015 meta-analysis, found that ginseng consumption is associated with a significantly decreased risk of cancer and that the effect is not organ-specific. A further study in 2021 confirmed that Ginseng may help prevent certain cancers. It is suggested that Ginseng is not consumed for more than one month, before taking a four-week break.

Green Tea; is known to be rich in polyphenols, and green and black teas have garnered interest for their cancer-preventative properties. Studies have shown that in populations where green tea consumption is high, such as in Japan, cancer rates tend to be lower. However, it is difficult to conclude from these observational studies whether tea is directly responsible for this effect.

Hemp seeds; the compound found in hemp seeds have shown potential anti-cancer effects. Hemp seeds are rich in omega-3 and omega-6 fatty acids, as well as important nutrients like vitamin E, magnesium, and protein, which all contribute to overall health. Some potential cancer-protective properties of hemp are thought to come from its ability to reduce inflammation and oxidative stress, both of which are linked to cancer development.

Turmeric; Curcumin has been studied in various preclinical settings, and early research has shown promising results. It appears to stop the growth of cancer cells and may prevent their spread by targeting multiple pathways involved in cancer development. However, like Hemp seeds, and other natural substances, the research is still in its infancy, and more clinical trials are needed to confirm its effectiveness in cancer prevention.

Chia seeds; mapping the genome of chia seeds, has been undertaken by Oregon University, which has opened up the potential for future research to more precisely target their beneficial compounds for treating conditions such as hypertension and cancer.

Flaxseeds; in the context of cancer prevention, are impressive. Some studies have demonstrated that 25g of flaxseed each day, may reduce tumour growth in both breast, and prostate cancers. Studies have also shown that it can enhance the effectiveness of Tamoxifen. It has a high fibre content which can contribute to reducing the risk of heart disease, and stroke by the promotion of healthy cholesterol levels.

These are just a few of the changes you can make to a well-balanced diet, alongside evidence-based treatments, which could offer additional protection against cancer.

Words of warning, however — do not rush out and obtain all of these natural substances. It is, essential to discuss with your doctor, before adding any of these to your diet.

Cancer is fundamentally a genetic disease, caused by changes or mutations in genes that control how our cells function, particularly in how they grow and divide. These genetic alterations can disrupt normal cell processes, leading to uncontrolled cell growth and the formation of tumours.

Under normal conditions, the body has mechanisms in place to eliminate cells with damaged DNA before they can become cancerous. However, as we age, the body's ability to detect and destroy these damaged cells diminishes. This decline in cellular surveillance contributes to the increased risk of cancer as we get older.

The relationship between ageing and cancer risk highlights the importance of early detection and prevention, as well as the need for ongoing research into how we can better understand and treat the genetic changes that lead to cancer. By strengthening our knowledge of these processes, we move closer to developing more effective treatments and prevention strategies for this disease.

Chapter 16
My Final Thoughts

In 1974, I was criss-crossing the country, driven by youthful energy and an insatiable passion for Hawkwind. Their music was my anthem, a pulsing soundtrack that felt like freedom itself. I'd stand among the crowd, the air thick with smoke and sweat, feeling the bass reverberate through my chest, as if the music were rewiring me, preparing me for a life beyond the mundane. Those adventures — nights spent on borrowed couches, hitching rides with strangers, and living on the thrill of the next show — were funded by my work at the Shipyard — a job that I knew, deep down, was not my destiny.

The clang of metal, the rhythm of hammer strikes, and the flash of the welder's torch, and the distant cries of gulls marked my days, but my mind was always elsewhere. I'd watch the ships taking shape, their hulls dark and massive, and imagined myself aboard one of them — an able seaman standing on deck, staring out at endless horizons.

Only a year after starting work in a local shipyard — following quiet discussions with my father, I had applied to join the Royal Navy. I pictured myself in uniform, standing tall with the wind in my face and the salt air filling my lungs. Discipline, discovery, the open sea — these would be my companions. I dreamed of foreign ports with their strange languages, sunrises in the middle of the ocean, and the kind of life that would make my hometown seem like a memory of another world.

But life, with its cruel irony, had other plans.

Just as I began to imagine a new chapter, the shadow of cancer took me in a deathly stranglehold. The diagnosis came like a storm cloud, obscuring the light. It tightened its grip, pulling me away from the dreams I had so carefully constructed. The Royal Navy, the adventures abroad, the life I thought I was destined for — all of it slipped away.

Sadly, before my application could even be considered, fate sailed me in a different direction.

Instead of salt air, I inhaled antiseptic. Instead of distant shores, I stared at syringes attacking my fragile veins. My body became a battleground, and I was forced to fight a war I had never enlisted for. Cancer became a harsh teacher;

forcing me to confront parts of myself I'd never known. It was a voyage of unheralded discovery, reshaping my life in ways that still reverberate today.

Here I stand, five decades after my diagnosis and, yet, even now, I often find myself wondering: what might have been? What if fate had not intervened so cruelly? What if I had set sail on the course I once envisioned? Would I have been happier? Might I have been braver? Could I have still found the lessons life had waiting for me, or would they have been lost in the noise of adventure?

I'll never know.

The path I imagined was never mine to walk. Instead, fate took me on a different journey — one filled with pain, yes, but also with unexpected revelations. I became a survivor, not of war or the sea, but of a battle within myself. But make no mistake, that voyage has been just as profound.

Still, on quiet nights, when the house is still and the echoes of a Lakota square hand drum plays hypnotically in my mind, I close my eyes and see that horizon. I see the ship I never boarded, the life I never lived. And I wonder — just for a moment — what might have been.

However, I am certain of one thing. Life is not a rehearsal, and we only have one chance to enjoy it.

The long pathway of life is fraught with obstacles; some large, some small, but all need to be jumped. When cancer knocked at my door, I had little idea how to deal with its psychological burden. The kaleidoscope of emotional turbulence that caused my mind to spin out of control resulted in my failure to manage the demons, or the ongoing dark thoughts following repeated treatment failures. The incomparable side effects that almost destroyed my feeble frame are memories that have moulded my personality today. Never will I forget how fortunate I am.

I am humbled, and honoured to have served as a senior haematology clinical nurse specialist, at the very top of the clinical nursing ladder. And, at the very hospital that established my cancer diagnosis half-a-century earlier.

In the strangest twist of fate, I found myself as the sole clinician performing bone marrow investigations at South Tyneside Hospital. Each time I carried out the procedure, I couldn't help but recall the day in 1975 when I was the one lying on the examination couch, bracing myself for the same invasive and painful ordeal.

However, after thirty-three years working in Oncology and Haematology, I decided, for several reasons, that the time was right to retire. My retirement brought sadness and I not only miss every component of my role but how I influenced, and was part of the care of so many incredible individuals, every one of them unique. Teaching nursing and medical staff on a whole range of cancer-related issues was also a real pleasure and an honour that I miss.

My health played a part in my final decision to retire. But, in addition, it was the change in management at South Tyneside NHS Foundation Trust, brought about when our hospital merged with another local Trust. The philosophy of the new management created anxiety and demoralization among staff, and their approach was so alien to what had gone before that I did not feel I wanted to be part of that new ethos.

Half-a-century ago, I was the frightened patient, mentally scarred and physically feeble. Then, forty years ago; I was the father of a child diagnosed with leukaemia, terrified as to what lay ahead. Only a few years ago, I was the nurse specialist, brimming with both confidence and pride — prescribing chemotherapy for those individuals with the same cancers as Donna and me.

Truly a life-changing roller-coaster ride like no other, but I would not change it for the world as my fate was woven into the tapestry of life when John and Ruby announced the arrival of their son in 1957. On several occasions, I almost grasped the irreversible handshake that suicide offered me, but, without the courage to complete that task, I suddenly realized that life is so short; it is a precious commodity unknown in its content, dimension and significantly its length.

Life is not a rehearsal, it is for living, it is a once-only opportunity to enjoy. Our future is uncertain; no one knows what lies ahead, what fate has planned. Therefore, live life fully, enjoy it as if each day were your last, one day it will be, and you should have no remorse to leave behind as I leave behind no remorse or regret. No one person can deny anyone else the opportunity to enjoy life to the best of their ability.

Never look back on your life unless you are prepared to smile and be reflective, never look forward unless you can dream. We all need dreams, and we all need hope. Life can be cruel, often difficult to negotiate, as I and many others have discovered, but it is there to be enjoyed, and it is our responsibility to do so.

That said, just being here, beating the odds is not without its challenges, as I have previously explained. I still endure moments when a cloak of darkness envelopes my thoughts, and I am plunged into an unexplained low mood. I say unexplained because life presently could not be sweeter, family life is good, I can recommend retirement, and we get to travel to America, at least once a year.

Yet, this unwanted plague of darkness occurs from time to time, even though June constantly tops up my glass, and usually, her eternal optimism and pragmatism is what gets me through. I still endure periods of negativity when uninvited darkness subverts my sanity, thoughts of further health failures, and a challenge to my mortality cloud my rational thought processes, thoughts that I struggle to control.

There is little doubt, in my mind, that this psychological burden hails back to my early days of diagnosis and my parent's collusion in trying to hide my illness from me.

But, more significantly, back in 1975, there was no Macmillan nurse. There was no clinical nurse specialist to deliver support the cancer patient.

The Cancer Reform Strategy (2007), placed an emphasis on providers of health-care that clinical nurse specialist's should have critical roles in the delivery, communication, and coordination of care and support. A nurse who must demonstrate a high level of skill, and knowledge, and who, significantly, improves the quality of care of a cancer patient, demonstrates leadership, and increases efficiency. Clearly, complex roles, as I know only too well from my practice — these roles, however, had not been thought of in the seventies.

Today, financial support packages are readily available to cancer patients; yet, these were non-existent during my illness — monetary support that can help support individuals with the hidden costs of a cancer diagnosis.

However, it is my view, that over and beyond financial support, psychological care is the fundamental element of help that can support patients to navigate the difficult pathway of cancer and its hidden network of obstacles. Sadly, it is my opinion, that some clinical nurse specialists lack the empathy and the knowledge to undertake these critical roles. A fact I have witnessed with '*my*' own eyes.

In today's modern NHS, the clinical nurse specialist should be working to empower individuals living with and beyond cancer. Patients should be supported as they adapt to life following the experience of prolonged and aggressive anticancer treatment that often last years and which can be characterized by not insignificant acute and long-term toxicities.

Although over 388,000 individuals are diagnosed with cancer each year, in the UK — in the past forty years, cancer survival rates have doubled. However, survivors need support for both long-term health-related consequences of treatment but, also, their psychological well-being.

The National Health Service is an unbelievable institution that we should be proud of and not take for granted. Cancer care has moved on since my diagnosis, not least with the emphasis on support and psychological care. It is not my intention to criticize the NHS. I have so much to thank it for, I simply seek to identify why, I remain troubled by the demons and memories of so long ago.

I truly believe it was that lack of support when both nurses and doctors were reluctant, or refused, to engage with the questions cancer patients asked about their disease and mortality. Of course, there will be other things that contributed, but that is a legacy I will take to my grave.

Surviving survivorship and becoming one of the longest-living cancer survivors is now the lifelong project that I continue to work on. In many respects, despite my advancing years, I feel life is just getting going, and I have so much more that I want to do and achieve. Who knows if I will have time to fulfil it all, but I intend to give it my best shot.

I am humbled, realizing my good fortune to still be around today, talking of my experience. Life truly is sweet.

At some point soon, I will re-visit Pine Ridge Indian Reservation and shake hands once again with the indigenous people that inspired me to overcome societies greatest, and perhaps most feared disease, cancer.

I will embrace the relatives of those that were my support throughout most, if not all, of my treatment, and yet they had no idea of who I was. Visiting Wounded Knee again will also happen, of that, there is no doubt. Our ongoing excursions to America and the hinterland of Montana will continue, which for June and me is heaven on earth.

Over the years, I have written dozens of articles for national and international nursing and medical press, presented lectures the length and breadth of the country on many aspects of haematology and cancer management. I am honoured to have won numerous awards both locally and nationally for my work in both oncology and haematology, yet, my greatest achievement is survival.

In 2021, Newcastle United was finally released from the stranglehold and fourteen-year ownership by a man who did not have the best interest of the club at heart — using the magpies to grow his financial empire. Hopefully, we, as long-suffering supporters, can, at last, look forward to the club moving forward with our new and visionary owners. I hope I will be around to see the dream come to fruition.

Amazingly, in the 2023/24 football season, Newcastle qualified to play against some of Europe's elite teams in the Champions League. In addition, they also played in the Carabao Cup Final, in February 2023, sadly getting beaten two goals to nil by Manchester United. And, I was there to see it all. Hopefully, just the start of our success.

Newcastle United also played in the Carabao Cup Final, in March 2025, and Newcastle beat Liverpool two goals to one — lifting our first domestic trophy in seventy years. As I stood among the faithful, and loyal supporters, tears of joy rolled down my cheeks.

More recently, and since retirement, I have started writing Children's fiction and my first two titles are now published. My third title, '**The Fastest Water Pistol in Splodge City**,' was published in September 2024.

In 2025, there will be at least, a further two titles that will hit the shelves, including '**Kingdom of Huckleberry Jam**'. And, all of these books, feature my grandson Daniel alongside yours truly, whom he refers to as Papa.

But, the most important aspect of life is truly that of family, especially the grandchildren, and we are blessed to have a supportive, and loving network of family both here in England and beyond. Many people claim to have found their soul-mate, the love of their life, I truly did. I am very fortunate that June is by my side and helping me to navigate the challenges of survivorship, including the lifelong psychological legacy it has bestowed upon me.

From clowning around at school to my deep love of rock music. From taking my first steps onto the employment ladder to crashing into a spiral of despair after my cancer diagnosis. From the unbearable side effects that led me to contemplate suicide to the euphoria of remission.

Then came the unthinkable — the devastating news that my daughter, Donna, had leukaemia. The helplessness of watching her suffer was unimaginable, yet so was the overwhelming joy when she, too, achieved remission against all odds.

The highs and lows continued — playing on stage at Donnington alongside members of Hawkwind, followed by a life-changing journey to South Dakota, where I met the Lakota Sioux at Pine Ridge Indian Reservation. In my darkest moments, they offered wisdom and healing that helped me find strength when I needed it most.

From battling chronic illness — including yet another cancer diagnosis — to finding pride in delivering nursing care at my hometown hospital, the very place where my diagnosis was first made fifty years earlier. And now, as I step into retirement, I embark on a new chapter — an award-winning children's author.

And so, my life goes on…

Nothing in this life is more important than family — they are a link to the past, and a connection to the future. One year before my father's death, he told me that his father, my grandfather, had told him during my illness that one day, he felt I would be a great man. Now, I could never be as great as either of them — grandad survived being captured by the Nazis, and was incarcerated as a prisoner of war during the First World War. Following his release, he returned to his family and worked the remainder of his life at Harton pit, as a miner. My father worked his entire life along the banks of the Tyne, and a kinder and more genuine man you could not wish to meet. But, if I died tomorrow, I can comfortably say, I have had a great life, but, I do not think or suggest that I am a great man.

Despite my earlier lack of focus in school and my tendency to play the fool rather than study, one particular moment stands out. In 1972, I wrote an essay on the oppression of the American Indian — a topic that, for some reason, resonated deeply with me — perhaps even then, fate was at play? To my surprise, I received an A-plus for the piece. It may have been the one and only time I fully applied myself to schoolwork, but it's a memory that still stands out.

Little did I know that connection to Native American history — especially the Lakota Sioux — would deepen into something far more personal and meaningful over the years. A reflection, and an awareness of how unknowingly, the indigenous people of the plains supported me.

In Chapter 5, I first mentioned the Lakota Sioux Nation when my Aunty Mary sent me a copy of 'Bury My Heart at Wounded Knee.' Later, in Chapter 7, I recounted my first face to face with an Indian, being photographed with a Native American (Cherokee), albeit, one who was dressed to attract tourists.

Fast-forward to 2024, my wife and I took our grandson Daniel to North Carolina. Among other things, we revisited Oconaluftee Village in the Smoky Mountains, retracing my steps from decades earlier — steps once filled with uncertainty and fragility. But, what made this trip particularly special was a photograph we took of Daniel with a Cherokee Indian, capturing a moment of connection that felt full circle in many ways.

It is the simple things in life, that surviving cancer offers to me, but also understanding that one day will, like everyone else, be my last.

For so many years, indeed, decades, I never knew my real self. But, when June came into my life, I knew then who John Walker Pattison really was. Deep down, the same person I had always been, just temporarily hidden beneath the surface of a shadow.

Completing my memoirs has been a cathartic experience, but I hope, more importantly, readers will be able to take some solace, and support from my story.

Finally, as the great wheel in the sky keeps on turning, no one knows where they will be tomorrow. But regardless of where that might be, my love and best wishes go out to you all, as I embark upon the next chapter in my life…

More information about John Walker Pattison is available at:-

https://johnwpattison.co.uk/